Managing Risk in Mortgage Portfolios

Managing Risk in Mortgage Portfolios

ALEX O. WILLIAMS

QUORUM BOOKS
NEW YORK
WESTPORT, CONNECTICUT
LONDON

Library of Congress Cataloging-in-Publication Data

Williams, Alex O., 1934–
  Managing risk in mortgage portfolios.

  Bibliography: p.
  Includes index.
  1. Mortgages.   2. Risk management.
3. Portfolio management.   I. Title.
HG4655.W55   1987   332.63'244   87-2497
ISBN 0-89930-058-8 (lib. bdg.   :   alk. paper)

British Library Cataloguing in Publication Data is available.

Library of Congress Catalog Card Number: 87-2497
ISBN: 0-89930-058-8

First published in 1987 by Quorum Books

Greenwood Press, Inc.
88 Post Road West, Westport, Connecticut   06881

Printed in the United States of America

The paper used in this book complies with the
Permanent Paper Standard issued by the National
Information Standards Organization (Z39.48-1984).

10 9 8 7 6 5 4 3 2 1

Contents

Part II: Risk Reduction Through Portfolio Diversification

Figures

Tables

Preface

Lenders always have to consider the risk of possible loss from delinquency and default when evaluating loan applications. Because of the long duration of mortgage loans, there is a higher risk of loss to the lender, since there is more time, and therefore more opportunity, for some form of financial adversity to occur that may inhibit the borrower's capacity to make the periodic mortgage service regularly and punctually.

To control its risk exposure over the life of the loan, lenders carry out a credit-scoring assessment of the likelihood of possible loss. A variety of methods and approaches are used to assess credit risk. These techniques range from simple numerical credit-scoring approaches that use only a few quantitative factors to more sophisticated methods incorporating advanced statistical and management science techniques.

This book presents a variety of the newer advanced statistical and management science techniques for controlling risk in a mortgage portfolio through screening out, at the time the application is made, potential borrowers assessed to have a higher likelihood of delinquency and default.

In chapter 1, a brief discussion is presented of how regulation was used to reduce risk in mortgage portfolios, the factors that led to the demise of the regulatory system, and the deregulated system.

The portfolio diversification approach to controlling risk in mortgage portfolios is developed in chapter 2. The expected value, standard deviation, and covariance are derived in the construction of a portfolio of two mortgage loans, with extension to portfolios of more than two loans. Portfolio analysis is a useful statistical tool through which the risk in a portfolio is spread out over different combinations of mortgages with low or negative covariance.

Chapter 3 presents the regression method of mortgage risk analysis and a breakdown of the four key characteristics of a mortgage loan: loan, borrower, property, and neighborhood.

The linear probability model is constructed in chapter 4 and applied to a set of data to demonstrate how it is used to measure both default and delinquency risks. In this model, the probability that a loan will be delinquent or will default is obtained directly from the data.

In chapter 5, a cohort analysis of delinquency risk is developed. The results of the analysis are presented and discussed. Cohort analysis has been shown to be a useful approach for analysis of government-sponsored Federal Housing Administration–Veterans Administration–type mortgages.

A discriminant functional analysis classification model is used to measure default risk in chapter 6. The factors are entered into the discriminant function in a stepwise manner, permitting only those factors that make a significant contribution in discriminating between good and bad loans to be included in the function. A holdout sample is then used to validate the discriminant function obtained by testing it on a data set other than the one on which it was developed.

In chapter 7, a procedure for constructing an index of loan quality is generated. An index is constructed for both foreclosed and delinquent loans. Credit-scoring instruments may be produced from an index for use by loan officers.

Chapter 8 presents an illustration of the process of evaluation of commercial and industrial properties. A hybrid combination of the income and the cash flow statements unique to real estate analysis, the "setup," is incorporated in the financial analysis. The net present value approach is then used to evaluate the after-tax cash flows, including cash flows from reversion.

Acknowledgments

The Operations Research techniques and research results presented in much of the book draw heavily from a national study commissioned by the Federal Savings and Loan Insurance Corporation and the Federal Home Loan Bank Board. These institutions are not responsible for the results reported here. I wish to thank Professors William Beranek, University of Georgia; George Von Furstenburg, Indiana University; David Pentico, Virginia Commonwealth University; and James Kenkel, and Robert Byrne (deceased), University of Pittsburgh for their collaboration in the study. Parts of chapter 6 on the application of discriminant function analysis are based on a research study by Professor T. Gregory Morton (deceased), University of Connecticut, in which he used data provided by banks and savings and loans located in Connecticut. I would like to express my gratitude for the useful comments made by my academic colleagues at Atlanta University and elsewhere who reviewed parts, or the whole draft, of the manuscript.

Many members of the staffs of the Federal Savings and Loan Insurance Corporation and the Federal Home Loan Bank Board made invaluable contributions to the national study. In particular, I wish to thank Richard Platt, former chairman of the Federal Home Loan Bank Board; Michael Westgate, Josephine McElhone, Harris Friedman, and Tom Zearley, former and current members of the Federal Home Loan Bank Board staff. Roger Lindland, former director of the Federal Savings and Loan Insurance Corporation provided valuable comments.

My gratitude is expressed to the presidents, vice presidents, and other members of the staff of the institutions who participated in the study. In particular, these institutions included First Federal Savings and Loan of Pittsburgh, Second Federal Savings and Loan of Pittsburgh, First Federal Savings and Loan of Homestead, Century Federal Savings and Loan of Pittsburgh, Parksdale Savings, Pioneer Savings and Loan of Bloomfield, and the Dollar Savings Bank. I am also grateful to many individuals in the Federal Home Loan Bank of Atlanta, the

Federal Home Loan Bank of Pittsburgh, the Department of Housing and Urban Development, Washington, D.C., and the Planning Department of the City of Pittsburgh.

Special acknowledgment is given to Atlanta University for its financial support for the preparation of this manuscript. The Atlanta University/Morehouse College Real Estate Institute provided organizational support.

My very special thanks go to Ms. Ethel Foureau, my assistant and Ms. Carol Mitchell, my secretary, for their tireless effort and assistance in preparing several drafts of the manuscript. Ms. Mary Ellen Raposa of the editorial staff at Greenwood Press did the final editing, making many suggestions for improving the clarity of the text. My thanks to Ms. Penny Sippel, the production editor, for her patience during my interminable delays, and for putting this book together. Finally, I offer my gratitude and appreciation to my family for their encouragement and support, and for the countless hours I spent away from them during the whole project.

PART I

The Environment: Regulation and the Mortgage Market

CHAPTER 1

The Etiology of Risk in Mortgage Portfolios

Lending institutions control risk in their mortgage portfolios through prescreening of loan applicants and through asset/liability management. The selection of loans to include in a portfolio dominated by long-term fixed rate loans basically involves the consideration of the underlying asset value and the stability and adequacy of the borrower's income to meet the periodic payments of principal, interest, taxes, and insurance (PITI) over the life of the loan. Asset/liability management, on the other hand, involves the matching, or synchronization, of the maturity of assets and liabilities through a maturity gap analysis approach.

The maturity gap analysis approach groups assets and liabilities by maturity categories and adjusts premiums accordingly. If, for example, three maturity categories are set up—less than one year, one to five years, and over five years—assets and liabilities are allocated to the three categories and determine the net maturity imbalance. This net imbalance determines the relative risk exposure.

The main thrust of this book involves the management of risk in the asset side of the balance sheet of mortgage institutions. This deals with the process of prescreening of loan applicants before the mortgage loan is made and the purchase and sale of loans and other securities in the asset portfolio.

To gain some insights into the etiology of risk in mortgage portfolios, it is helpful to examine the regulations within which lending institutions operated until the early 1980s when the deregulation of depository institutions removed many of the regulatory constraints. This background will illuminate some of the current problems involved in managing risk in mortgage portfolios.

REGULATION AND MORTGAGE PORTFOLIO RISK

The mortgage industry has been regulated since the early 1930s when the federal home loan bank system was created and the Federal Savings and Loan

Insurance Corporation (FSLIC) established. Federal regulation created the structure of the mortgage industry, controlled mortgage portfolio risk in the savings industry, and provided three decades of relative stability in the mortgage market with minimal risk in institutional mortgage portfolios. The following sections trace the developments during the period of regulation, the policies and instruments of regulation, and their impact on controlling risk in institutional mortgage portfolios.

The focus is on regulation of the savings industry, where Congress placed the primary responsibility for providing mortgage financing. Commercial banks and other financing institutions such as insurance companies and pension funds are actively involved in mortgage financing. The discussion that follows in this chapter, and the models and analysis of mortgage loans presented in the rest of the book, are equally applicable to their mortgage-lending activities.

Housing Policy

The major housing shortage in the urban areas following World War I attracted Congress' attention to the savings and loan industry as the providers of home mortgage credit, and in 1919 a bill was introduced in the Senate to create a Federal Home Loan Board and Home Loan Banks for the ''Purpose of Aiding and Financing the construction of homes.'' This bill is recognized as the first attempt to set up a national housing policy, culminating in the Federal Home Loan Bank Act of 1932.

Whereas the focus of housing policy prior to the Great Depression had been to expand the housing supply through construction of new housing, the focus shifted in the 1930s to the plight of existing homeowners experiencing record default rates of up to 50 percent on outstanding mortgages. Congress enacted the Home Owners' Loan Act of 1933 to achieve two immediate objectives: (1) The Home Owners' Loan Corporation was authorized to acquire and refinance individual homeowners' mortgages, the origin of the secondary mortgage market; and (2) the Federal Home Loan Bank Board (FHLBB) was authorized to charter federal savings and loan associations in part to enable the one-third of the counties nationwide with home mortgage–lending facilities to start up institutions in their localities. In 1934 Congress passed legislation creating a government-sponsored corporation, the Federal Savings and Loan Insurance Corporation, to insure accounts at savings and loans and to restore public confidence in the federal home loan bank systems.

The Federal Home Loan Bank System

In the wake of the financial crisis of the 1930s, the financial depository industry was radically transformed through congressional legislation to produce a nonbank federal regulatory system for savings institutions that remained intact until the early 1980s. Three pieces of legislation developed the federal home loan system: The Federal Home Loan Bank Act of 1932 established the Federal Home Loan Bank Board and a system of 12 district federal home loan banks to provide liquidity for the mortgage portfolios of savings and loans. The powers of the FHLBB were extended by the Home Owners' Loan Act of 1933 to cover chartering and regulating savings and loan associations. The National Housing Act of 1934 established the FSLIC to insure the savings deposits of savings and loan associations.

The regulatory structure of the federal home loan system is comparable with the structure of the commercial bank system. Since all deposit intermediaries compete for the same pool of savings, a regulatory balance had to be maintained in order not to provide unintentional advantage to either system that might drive the other out of the money market. Because of the activities proscribed by the National Housing Act of 1934, savings and loans were restricted to fixed rate long-term loan portfolios financed with short-term deposit liabilities. The spread between the long-term rates on mortgage loans and the short-term interest rates paid on deposit liabilities produced the real source of income for these institutions. Loan origination and servicing fees made up for much of the other sources of income. The asset/liability structure of savings and loans was designed to yield profitable returns in an environment of interest rate stability. The liquidity preference theory postulates that with interest rate stability, the spread between long- and short-term interest rates will be constant or even positive at all times, and the prevalence of a normal yield curve can be seen to persist over long periods of time. Savings institutions were operated under the regulatory constraints with the knowledge that the government was also responsible for (1) the slope of the yield curve, through the policies of the Federal Reserve Board; and (2) insuring savings and loans through the FSLIC. The savings industry enjoyed fairly stable interest rates over the 30-year period from 1935 to 1965, when the yield curve had a relatively normal slope.

Regulation Q and Risk Reduction in Mortgage Portfolios

Reflecting the regulatory constraints under which they operated, the balance sheet of savings and loans was made up of very long-term assets, essentially of fixed rate mortgage loans, and short-term liabilities composed of deposits. In a stable interest rate environment, the slope of the yield curve is normal, with long-term rates higher than short-term rates. By earning a higher return on long-term assets than the interest cost on short-term deposit liabilities, these institutions were able to maintain profitability. Rising short-term interest rates reduce the spread between the long-term rates on assets and the higher short-term rates on liabilities, thus reducing profitability. As short-term rates increase relative to long-term rates, profitability falls; the alternative facing the savings industry is either to curtail lending or to find other less costly sources of funds for the loans on its books.

Two actions were taken by the U.S. Congress and implemented by the regulatory agencies to alleviate the interest rate problems facing the savings industry. First, ceilings were placed on interest rates that savings and loans and commercial banks could pay to depositors. This action, known in the industry as "Regulation Q," had the effect of limiting the extent to which lenders had to compete for funds and significantly reduced the cost of funds to the institutions. The rate ceilings on the interest that depository institutions could pay on deposits restricted their ability to compete for deposits. Second, savings and loans were permitted to pay a slightly higher ceiling rate on deposits than commercial banks, to enable them to attract an adequate amount of deposits, since they did not have checking accounts at the time.

By capping the rate of interest that savings and loans and commercial banks could pay, the interest rate ceilings under Regulation Q in effect constrained the depository institutions' ability to compete for funds during a period of rising short-term interest rates. The result was that consumers increasingly shifted their deposits from commercial banks and savings and loans to money market funds, paying higher rates of interest without any limiting constraints. Consumers transferred their funds to higher-paying money market funds in an effort to hedge against a rising inflation rate, resulting in disintermediation for commercial banks and savings and loans. Three disintermediation episodes occurred in the 1960s and 1970s that caused significant reduction in the rate of inflow of savings to savings institutions in contrast to withdrawal of funds from commercial banks.

Regulation Q proved to be a rather ineffective policy instrument for stabilizing the flow of funds in commercial banks and savings institutions. The President's Commission on Financial Structure and Deregulation (1971) and the Congressional Study of Financial Institutions and the National Economy (1976) both made recommendations to change the current regulatory policy and the existing system.

DEREGULATION AND RISK CHANGES IN MORTGAGE PORTFOLIOS

The Depository Institutions Deregulation and Monetary Control Act (DIDMCA) of 1980 and 1982 effectively removed most of the regulatory restrictions on the asset and liability structure of depository institutions. This ended the regulatory structure created in the 1930s. The demise of Regulation Q effectively removed the protection of the earnings of depository institutions by the institution of interest rate ceilings. While the removal of Regulation Q solved the disintermediation problem, it brought back the risks from interest rate variability on deposit liabilities. Earnings were squeezed as interest rates trended upward. The need arose to supply relief by providing flexibility in the asset structure by removal of regulations limiting the maturities and type of loans in the asset structure and the variability of interest rates charged on these loans. It also became necessary to expand the liability structure to permit new deposit instruments to meet the changing needs of consumer and commercial depositors. The enactment of DIDMCA provided the regulatory relief necessary for depository institutions to manage their portfolios effectively.

Demise of Regulation Q and an End to Protection

Interest rates became increasingly volatile in the late 1960s and throughout the 1970s, and it was evident that the present system for housing finance could not function adequately during periods of instability of interest rates. As interest rates increased in the second half of the 1970s, the savings institutions were again faced with a serious threat of disintermediation. In 1978, as the prospect of disintermediation on a massive scale increased with rising interest rates, significant new powers were given depository institutions in June to issue, for the first time, money market certificates in minimum denominations of $10,000 at rates slightly above the prevailing six-month U.S. Treasury bill rate. The money market certificates were in direct competition with the money market funds. Combined with the added security of the FSLIC deposit insurance, the certificates gained ready acceptance and popularity among depositors, and by summer 1979, approximately 20 percent of all saving deposits at savings and loans were in six-month money market certificates.

The interest rates on money market certificates were tied to the Treasury bill rate and floated directly with it. Thus ended an era of protection of the earnings through Regulation Q. Increases in the level of interest rates during 1979, 1980, and 1981 severely squeezed the profit margin of savings institutions, causing significant losses and the threat of insolvency.

Depository Institutions Deregulation and Monetary Control Act of 1980

Significant changes in the market environment made it necessary that savings and loan associations be empowered to offer a wider range of deposit instruments and asset securities to enable them to compete more effectively in the money markets and to manage their asset structure more efficiently. Congress enacted DIDMCA in 1980.

Table 1.1 presents the key features of DIDMCA for changes in the asset/liability structure of federally chartered savings and loan associations. DIDMCA 1980 provided for changes in the asset structure: to expand real estate loan portfolios to include commercial real estate loans, to enter the consumer loan market and credit card lending, and to engage in commercial paper investments. Savings and loans were provided with a broader range of lending and investment activity to reduce their dependence on residential mortgages.

Changes in the liability structure include the authority to establish interest-bearing (NOW) checking accounts for individuals, a key provision removing an important disadvantage of savings and loans to commercial banks and providing a major source of liquidity. The imposition of reserve requirements provides

Table 1.1
**Depository Institutions Deregulation and Monetary Control Act of 1980: Impact
on Asset/Liability Structure of Federally Chartered Savings and Loan
Associations**

Changes in Asset Structure	Impact on Portfolio
Empowerment to issue	
- Commercial real estate loans	
	- Broaden mortgage portfolio
- Consumer loans	
	- Increase short- and medium-term variable rate instruments
- Investments in commercial paper (up to 20 percent of assets	
- Credit card lending	

Changes in Liability Structure	Impact
- Interest-bearing checking accounts for individuals and nonprofit customers	- Checking accounts increase liquidity, broaden sources
- Reserve requirements for transaction accounts and nonpersonal time deposits	- Provide protection, reduce liquidity
- Trust activities	- Increase investable funds, broaden sources

Source: Depository Institutions Deregulation and Monetary Control Act of
          1980 [Public Law 96, 221, 94 stat. 132 (1980)].

protection for depositors but reduces liquidity since the reserve cannot be loaned
out. The power to engage in trust activities provides a useful source of investable
funds.

DIDMCA finally provided for the full entry of thrift institutions into the
payments system by authorizing NOW accounts for individuals and nonprofit
customers of thrift institutions. Another key feature is the phaseout of deposit
rate capacity to diversify the asset structure further through commercial real
estate loans, consumer loans, investments in commercial paper, and other corporate debt securities.

Garn–St. Germain Depository Institutions Act of 1982

Table 1.2 presents the features of the Garn–St. Germain Depository Institutions Act of 1982 (GSGDIA) and its impact on the asset/liability structure of federally chartered savings and loans. Its enactment further expanded the deregulatory thrust of DIDMCA 1980, giving broader powers to federally chartered savings and loans. New asset authorizations include commercial real estate

Table 1.2
Garn–St. Germain Depository Institutions Act of 1982: Impact on Federally Chartered Savings and Loan Asset/Liability Structure

Changes in Asset Structure	Impact
– Eliminates restricted loan-to-value ratios on residential mortgage loans	– Increases mortgage credit risk
– Commercial real estate loans (up to 40 percent of assets)	– Broaden further commercial mortgage activity
– Investment in commercial paper	– Broadens commercial investment
– Corporate debt securities (up to 100 percent of assets)	– Broadens commercial investment
– Consumer loans (up to 30 percent of assets)	– Increase consumer loan activity
– Personal property leasing (up to 10 percent of assets)	– Expansion to automobile leasing and residential property

Changes in Liability Structure	
– Demand deposit for business customers	– Increase liquidity
– New money market deposit accounts to compete with money market funds	– Increase liquidity
– Net worth certificates for purchase by FSLIC	– Increase liquidity
– DeNovo Federal Stock Associations	– Funds from stock sales

Source: Garn–St. Germain Depository Institutions Act of 1982 [Public Law 97–320, 96 stat. 1469 (1982)].

loans, a lucrative source for lending especially in commercial office development in suburban areas and redevelopment of downtown offices in metropolitan areas. Powers to invest in commercial papers and corporate debt securities up to 100 percent of assets provide maximum investment flexibility when real estate markets are down. Consumer loans are limited to 30 percent of assets, a ceiling high enough to permit restructuring of the asset portfolio. There is also authorization to engage in personal property leasing such as automobile leasing, a growing market area. With the flexibility to restructure assets with less dominance from residential fixed mortgage loans, the asset portfolio risk is reduced to some degree. The savings and loans are required to eliminate the restrictive loan-to-value (L/V) ratios on residential mortgage loans requiring substantial down payments. The higher L/V ratios increase the riskiness of mortgage credit.

All the changes in the liability structure expanded the sources of deposits, thereby increasing the liquidity of the savings and loans. With the expanded variety of sources, the savings and loans can top different sources at different interest rates.

By permitting thrifts to offer checking accounts, money market deposit accounts, and super NOW accounts, the GSGDIA further expanded the capacity of savings and loans to compete with money market funds. The only depositors not able to receive explicit interest on transaction deposits were corporate customers.

OUTLOOK FOR THE SAVINGS INDUSTRY

The regulatory changes presented above have essentially removed many of the barriers that have separated savings and loans from commercial banks. The regulatory constraints on the structure of the assets and liabilities of savings and loans have been significantly relaxed, and management now has greater flexibility in synchronizing the durations of assets and liabilities in their balance sheets.

Savings and loans' management faces greater competition in the deregulated financial services industry from commercial banks, with whom they are now in head-to-head competition, and from nonbank financial intermediaries such as insurance companies, pension funds, and the growing extraindustry competition from major U.S. corporations now offering retail and wholesale services.[1]

The thrifts face new competition in their traditional mortgage-lending business, which will increase the competitive pressure in their asset structure in the next few years. These institutions had been constrained in the past to make only long-term fixed rate mortgage loans and fund them with short-term deposits that increase their interest rate risks. The savings and loans want to restructure their loan portfolio to reduce their interest rate exposure by making variable rate mortgages with shorter maturity. At the same time, competing investors like insurance companies with long-term liabilities are in a better position to acquire long-term fixed rate mortgages without any increase in their interest rate exposure. The savings and loans face the risk of losing market share in the mortgage-lending business as shorter-term flexible rate mortgages, which shift the interest rate risk to the borrower, are substituted for fixed rate mortgages.

The new markets open to savings and loans from the deregulations are already very competitive. Commercial and consumer lending businesses have been highly competitive markets that require a high level of management expertise. Management skills need to be upgraded as necessary for them to compete on a par with the other institutions that have been operating in these markets for a long time.

MANAGING MORTGAGE PORTFOLIO RISK IN A DEREGULATED ENVIRONMENT

DIDMCA removed most of the regulatory restrictions on the asset/liability structure by expanding the types of loans, investments, and deposits that depository institutions could engage in and provided flexibility in interest rates to include variable rates on assets as well as liabilities. The transformation of savings institutions, in particular savings and loan associations, has been dramatic.

The upshot of deregulation is the head-to-head, direct competition of commercial banks and savings institutions, a situation that regulation successfully kept under control until now. While greater competition is healthy for the economy, it significantly increases risk, particularly in the mortgage portfolio. Savings institutions are now empowered to make new types of loans, for example, commercial loans, that require different managerial skills. Floating rate loans on residential mortgages where the borrower's income is from wages or salaries introduce a potentially very serious risk of default when wages and salaries do not rise as fast as interest rates increase within very short periods.

Managing the expanded asset and liability structure in a flexible interest rate environment demands greater managerial capacity and efficiency. It requires the use of modern tools and techniques of financial management provided by the management science methods currently available and those that will become available in the future, to keep management on the forefront of the latest developments. The use of the computer is mandatory to utilize statistical and scientific modeling techniques, as well as for bookkeeping and accounting operations. A few of the management science and statistical models are presented in this book to demonstrate to management how they can be used to help in the selection.

THE MORTGAGE MARKET

This section presents a brief survey of the mortgage market, before the discussion of mortgage credit risk in the next section.

There are two types of mortgage markets: the primary mortgage market and the secondary mortgage market. The primary mortgage market deals with the initiation of mortgages to finance the purchase and sale of tangible property. The secondary market involves the buying and selling of existing mortgage loans and mortgage securities to increase liquidity and to change the risk configuration in the portfolio.

The Primary Mortgage Market

Because the mortgaged property is location specific and cannot be moved, the configuration and dimension of the mortgage market are important since location is an important risk factor.

The primary mortgage market is made up of a large number of local mortgage markets spread throughout the urban areas and rural communities of the United States. Since this market involves the purchase and sale of tangible property, it tends to be location specific; that is, it is described by the real estate activities of each community.

The primary market can be delineated into residential, farm, and commercial and industrial sectors. The nature of mortgage risk in each sector is distinguishable from that in the other sectors.

Residential Mortgage Market

The residential market is generally the largest, in terms of volume and value, in most communities. Because of its size, it is usually the most active market in terms of turnover of existing units and construction of new units. The demand for mortgage loans in this sector of the primary market is normally high, and the total dollar value of mortgage loans is correspondingly high relative to the other sectors.

The residential mortgage market can be further delineated in terms of single-family and multifamily properties. Single-family units make up the preponderance of mortgage activity in the residential market.

Mortgage loans on residential property are generally of two types: conventional and U.S. government guaranteed [Federal Housing Administration (FHA) and Veterans Administration (VA)]. This breakdown reflects the loan manager's assessment of the riskiness of the borrower at the time the loan is originated.

Farm Mortgage Market

The farm mortgage market comprises all farm properties located in the rural areas and suburban fringes of metropolitan areas. The farm market is identified separately because of its special nature. Farming is a business based upon the agricultural output of a farm. The mortgage is secured by the value of the farm, with the income generated paying off the mortgage. Farm mortgage is therefore similar to commercial mortgage. Farm production, however, is to a great extent dependent upon weather and other ecological conditions.

Technological advances have created the need for massive agricultural farming operations to take advantage of the built-in economies of scale of the equipment and chemical agents. Farms are rapidly being transformed into large-scale units, and the family farm appears to be threatened.

Commercial and Industrial Mortgage Markets

The commercial mortgage loan market includes financing for the purchase and sale of new and existing office buildings and office complexes, shopping malls, shopping centers, and other commercial units. The industrial mortgage market deals with the purchase and sale of new and existing manufacturing plants and facilities.

Area Participations

Participations have become the most common form of secondary market activity for savings institutions because this vehicle requires that the seller service and retain an ownership in a portion of the loan(s) sold. There are three categories of participation: (1) participations within an institution's lending territory, (2) participations outside an institution's lending territory, and (3) participations in nationwide loans.

The Secondary Mortgage Market and Institutional Liquidity

The secondary mortgage market provides for liquidity in mortgage portfolios. Before the secondary mortgage market was created, an association had virtually to carry its mortgage loans on its books until they were paid up, or at maturity. The sale of mortgages between institutions was rather infrequent and required special bilateral arrangements. Institutional portfolios were consequently rather illiquid. Whole loans, as well as pools of loans, are packaged and sold in the secondary mortgage market to generate new lending funds. The ability to sell off portions of a mortgage portfolio provides a degree of flexibility for portfolio managers to restructure their portfolios from time to time. The secondary mortgage market is therefore of significant importance to the mortgage industry.

The Urban Mortgage Market

The urban mortgage market is a significant subset of the national mortgage market. The changes in the components of the urban mortgage market reflect existing conditions and activities taking place within the urban area, the surrounding metropolitan areas, and the national economic climate. The urban market is a dynamic entity that includes population shifts such as in-migration and out-migration to and from the cities to suburban areas and other parts of the country.

The urban mortgage market can be divided into several grid areas representing neighborhoods with different characteristics reflecting different risk complexions. These include the blighted ghetto areas, a result of overcrowding, lack of employment opportunities, absence of business and industry, instability of income, and other economic conditions that leave the area with little or no economic viability. Other parts of the city may also appear to have the same type of income constraints and absence of viable economic activity that presage degeneration of the locality with an accompanying reduction in property values. Stable neighborhoods and the growing outer areas form the rest of the city.

The economic health and viability of the metropolitan area are significant factors in analyzing and determining the risks associated with mortgage lending in the urban area. A vibrant economic environment produces a degree of stability in both social and economic factors in the home, lowers layoff and unemployment rates, creating income stability in the household units within the area. On the other hand, a stagnant economic environment cannot support demographic growth, and prolonged economic decline will generate decay. The economic environment of the metropolitan area as reflected by the type of industrial and commercial activities undertaken has significant implications for the risks inherent in mortgage lending in urban areas.

In the metropolitan area, there are mortgages on income property, including multifamily complexes and business properties, and homes. The risks in mortgages made on business property are perceived to be of a different nature than those on residential property.

CONSUMER LOANS

In addition to mortgage loans, lending institutions carry consumer loans in their loan portfolios. These include mobile home loans, home improvement loans (conventional and government insured), loans secured by savings accounts, educational loans, and all other loans. Because a mobile home can be moved from place to place, it is treated as a vehicular unit and classified as a consumer loan.

Home improvement loans are normally secured by a second mortgage on the residential unit being improved. The FHA provides guarantees for borrowers that do not meet the standards for conventional loans.

A significant proportion of consumer loans are secured by the borrowers' savings accounts. These loans are taken out to meet a variety of needs.

Educational loans are made under a variety of federal programs carrying federal government guarantees.

Other loans include automobile and other personal-type loans. These have increased significantly as a proportion of total consumer loans. The Depository Institutions Deregulation and Monetary Control Acts of 1980 and 1982 authorized savings institutions to make credit card loans and an increase in the percentage of their assets attributable to consumer loans.

RISK IN MORTGAGE LENDING

The quality of mortgage credit has been of interest to institutions involved in mortgage lending, and continuing efforts have been made to ascertain and measure the underlying factors of mortgage credit quality.[2] The risk in mortgage lending can be viewed in terms of the borrower, the mortgage, the property, the neighborhood, or the lender.

The lender's risk is the probability of dollar loss resulting from the variability in the earnings stream of the lending institution. Two general cases can be delineated in this regard. In the first case are the institutions experiencing high rates of growth that may be due to one of the following three cases or some combinations of the three.

Case 1.1. An aggressive savings policy, in which the institution pays above-normal interest rates to attract marginal savers. Such a policy leads to a narrowing of the spread between income and payments, thereby reducing net earnings. The extent to which net earnings is reduced may indicate the degree of risk exposure.

Case 1.2. An aggressive mortgage policy, in which the institution proceeds to make high-risk loans by charging high interest rates to compensate for the risk. The higher the rate charged, the greater the perceived risk and the higher the probability of default.

Case 1.3. An aggressive growth and expansion policy through external forces, via acquisition of fledgling institutions. The resulting portfolio may have more risk exposure, and the earnings stream from the new portfolio may be more volatile. The experiences of these institutions may be the result of past policies of the varieties in case 1.1 above and may need corrective measures.

In discussing the probability of loss, it is essential to distinguish between the assessment of risk based on information in the lender's hands at the time the mortgage, or loan, is made versus the explanation for the loss realized at some future time. The risk perceived, and undertaken, at the time the loan is granted can be measured by those aspects of the credit transaction known to be associated with risk: the credit terms such as the loan-to-value ratio and the maturity, as well as borrower characteristics such as the payment-to-income (P/I) ratio, occupation, etc. The ex post explanation of the loss is a retrospective assessment of what caused the adverse experience of the loan as indicated by delinquency, slow loan, or foreclosure. The realization of loss of income or principal can be explained in light of changing economic, demographic, and social characteristics.

A deterioration of loan quality may be recognized in several ways: (1) a decline in actual quality, as indicated by delinquency and foreclosure rates reported after the event; (2) a decline in estimated quality, which may first be indicated by above-normal interest rate loans or appraisals and reserves ordered by examiners for the Federal Savings and Loan Insurance Corporation or the Federal Deposit Insurance Corporation; (3) a shift toward types of mortgages expected to involve higher delinquency or foreclosures; or (4) a change for the worse in the economic prospects of a significant number of borrowers.

The risks in mortgages made on business property are a function of the income-generating ability of the business and the stability of the income stream, both of which are dependent on the economic viability of the metropolitan area or region and to some extent on the national economic picture. The risk in mortgages on business property results from the inability of the business to generate adequate cash flow to service the mortgage loan, potentially resulting in delinquency and foreclosure.

The risks inherent in residential mortgage lending are perceived to be those of default and delinquency. Delinquency risk may be delineated into two subcategories: delinquency and serious delinquency, technically referred to as "slow loans."

Residential mortgage risk may be viewed in terms of the personal characteristics of the mortgagor, including the domestic circumstances, the asset in the mortgage indenture, the various factors influencing the mortgagor's environment (both social and demographic), and the economic vitality of the area in which the house is located. In addition, there is also the risk attached to the value of the asset itself, from the age and architectural design of the house, which determines its marketability, and the prospective price movements of real estate in the local market.

ASSESSING MORTGAGE CREDIT RISK

To evaluate commercial credit, risk credit managers use the five C's of credit: character, capacity, capital, collateral, and conditions. Character deals with the probability that the borrower will honor obligations to pay the debt. Capacity measures the mortgagor's ability to repay the mortgage loan. Capital reflects the tangible net worth of the borrower, while collateral refers to the mortgaged asset. Conditions relate to the impact of general economic trends or areas of the economy on the borrower's ability to repay the debt obligation.

The five C's of credit risk are directly applicable to the assessment of mortgage risk and used as the basis for identifying explanatory factors and for the construction and development of management science and statistical models. Mortgage loans are normally made for very long periods of time, in contrast to general commercial credit, and mortgaged asset is location specific and has very high values relative to the income capacity of the mortgagor. These differences increase the complexity of mortgage credit risk and require a larger number of explanatory factors and more sophisticated modeling techniques than normal commercial credit of much shorter duration. All other things given, the longer the life of the loan, the greater is the risk exposure since there is more time for things to go wrong.

The empirical applications of the models presented in this book are based on studies designed to provide management with insights into what social, economic, and demographic factors affect, or do not affect, credit risk in mortgage lending primarily in metropolitan areas and contiguous rural areas. Multiple regression and discriminate function models are used in the analysis of the empirical data.

The analysis utilizes a neighborhood approach based upon the hypothesis that the urban area and its immediate suburban areas can be delineated into neighborhoods on the basis of a number of social, economic, and demographic variables, such as income, unemployment rates, racial and ethnic compositions, crime rates, etc., that give them separate distinctive identifying characteristics. Neighborhoods with certain characteristics become desirable and very attractive to home buyers. The demand for homes in such a neighborhood will rise, and home prices will be bid up as demand outstrips supply. Since this type of neighborhood will tend to show growth in property valuation, it is expected that mortgage quality will be high.

Neighborhoods with poor characteristics will be less desirable or even undesirable. Residents will become unhappy and desire change, thereby moving out. Such a neighborhood will be less able to attract home buyers, except for minority and low-income groups. It is expected that certain identifiable characteristics contribute to a deterioration in mortgage quality.

PREVIOUS STUDIES

Several studies on the quality of mortgage credit have been done using various techniques ranging from cross-classification analysis to multiple regression techniques. Many useful insights were gained from these studies that are helpful in various ways. These studies have, for the most part, treated mortgages in the aggregate, either for the whole economy, for a region, or across the country covered by a particular insurance type such as FHA or VA. The findings of these studies are useful in terms of the objectives they were intended to meet.[3] By grouping all mortgages in a region or across the country together, these studies ignored any differences that may exist between the social and economic conditions of the rural areas and those of the urban scene.

The cities are the main commercial and industrial centers. The city and the surrounding municipalities provide the residential areas for the supporting work forces of the commercial and industrial centers. As a result, the housing and mortgage markets of the metropolitan areas are important subsets of the national mortgage market, with significant distinguishing characteristics that make it desirable for them to be studied as separate entities.

The problems of decay in the urban environment have been brought into sharp focus in the last decade or so. The impact of discrimination and the resulting ghetto formation on housing and housing prices has been dramatic at times, creating uncertainty and affecting the mortgage quality of lending institutions. An exodus of white and black city dwellers to the suburbs has had a compounding effect on mortgage quality. All of these transformations indicate the need for a closer look at the urban metropolitan mortgage market and an assessment of the quality of mortgage credit as it exists and could be expected to perform if there were a higher level of lending in these areas.

NOTES

1. These include a wide range of both retail and wholesale services including commercial finance, consumer and real estate lending, insurance leasing, investment and brokerage, business and personal services, and payment services.

2. See Federal Home Loan Bank Board, *Agenda for Reform* (Washington, D.C.: United States Government Printing Office, March 1983), p. 39.

3. See references following.

REFERENCES

Herzog, John P., and Earley, James S. *Home Mortgage Delinquency and Foreclosure.* New York: Columbia University Press for National Bureau of Economic Research, 1970.

Jones, O., and Grebler, L. *The Secondary Mortgage Market.* Los Angeles: Real Estate Research Program, University of California, 1961.

Jung, Allen F. "Terms on Conventional Mortgage Loans on Existing Homes." *Journal of Finance* (1962): Vol. 17, pp. 432–43.

Klaman, Saul B. *The Postwar Residential Mortgage Market.* Princeton: Princeton University Press for National Bureau of Economic Research, 1961.

Moore, Geoffrey H. "The Quality of Credit in Booms and Depressions." *Journal of Finance* (1956): Vol. XI., pp. 288–300.

Morton, I. E. *Urban Mortgage Lending: Comparative Markets and Experience.* Princeton: Princeton University Press for National Bureau of Economic Research, 1956.

Von Furstenberg, George. "Default Risk on FHA-Insured Home Mortgages as a Function of the Terms of Financing—A Quantitative Analysis." *Journal of Finance* (1969): Vol. 24, pp. 459–77.

PART II

Risk Reduction Through Portfolio Diversification

CHAPTER 2

Controlling Risk in Mortgage Portfolios

This chapter deals with the process of managing risk in the mortgage portfolio. Risk arises because of fluctuations in the cash flows, resulting in volatility in the net income or return. In this sense, risk may be described as the probability of realizing loss in the mortgage portfolio. It is therefore important to gain a full understanding of the nature of risk in a portfolio before proceeding to deal with the process of managing the risk.

We will first develop an example of investing in safe and risky undertakings with the aid of the planting of crops. The risk profile of each type of crop will be examined and the risky crops combined in portfolios to demonstrate how these combinations may be safer to the farmer than any single crop. The crop example is parallel to the investing process, and it shows how risky investments can be combined in a portfolio that is safer than any single investment.

Consideration is then given to the measurement of risk in a portfolio. Since the assets in a portfolio move in relation to each other, the risk of an asset can be measured by its co-movement with the other assets in the portfolio. One way of measuring the asset's co-movement is by regressing the asset's returns on the portfolio's returns to obtain the coefficient for the slope of the regression for β, where β is the systematic risk of the asset in relation to the portfolio in which the asset is situated.

A farmer can be considered an investor. He invests his money and time in farming, which, if he so chose, could be invested in alternative pursuits that might generate income with, perhaps, relatively less risk. In today's economy, there is agribusiness in which the investor is not necessarily a farmer. There is also the commodities futures market, an integral part of the financial markets. The investor chooses to invest in farming in preference to investing in any other kind of business or in the securities market. The crop example, as one investment alternative, is therefore an appropriate illustration.

RISK AND RETURN IN PORTFOLIOS

A rational economic person will always want to earn a positive income, or return, in every economic endeavor. In other words, the person will try to minimize or avoid realizing negative income, or negative return. Such behavior is described as the inclination to be "risk averse." When faced with a choice, a risk-averse person will always prefer investments with certain outcomes to investments whose outcomes are uncertain, otherwise called "risky investments." The concepts of certain (or safe) and risky are illustrated with the aid of a crop example.

> *Case 2.1.* A farmer has a certain acreage of land, which can be planted with one crop or a variety of crops. The farmer can plant soybeans, peanuts, grapes, and peaches. The yield (in bushels) per acre depends upon the amount of rainfall. The crop yield at various levels of rainfall is given in table 2.1.

It would be difficult to tell offhand, if at all, which of the crops is the safest and which is the riskiest without some information on the variation of rainfall. For example, if rainfall varies within the range of 10 to 50 inches a season, soybeans are just as safe as peanuts; and since soybeans produce a higher yield, they are a safe and abundant crop. While peanuts are safe at any rainfall level, their productivity is constant, however. Grapes and peaches would be considered risky crops in this range of rainfall, because with rainfall above 40 inches, their yield falls to zero. If, on the other hand, the range of rainfall is 5 to 40 inches a year, soybeans become a risky crop, since their yield is zero at rainfall below 10 inches. In contrast, grapes and peaches are safer crops, while peanuts remain a safe crop. It is clear that additional information on rainfall would help in the determination of which crop is risky and which is safe. In table 2.2 is presented a likelihood distribution of rainfall.

Table 2.1
Crop Yield in Bushels at Various Levels of Rainfall

CROP (C)	R A I N F A L L (R)				
	<10 inches	10–25 inches	25–40 inches	40–55 inches	>55 inches
Soybean	0	15	36	50	66
Grape	21	30	20	10	0
Peanut	20	20	20	20	20
Peach	45	21	10	6	0

Table 2.2
Rainfall Distribution and Likelihood

	R_1	R_2	R_3	R_4	R_5
Rainfall (R)	<10 inches	10–25 inches	25–40 inches	40–55 inches	>55 inches
Likelihood (P)	15%	20%	35%	20%	10%

The Riskless Case

A riskless crop is one whose yield does not vary with fluctuations in the amount of rainfall. In the example above, peanuts are the riskless crop since their yield remains at 20 bushels over all ranges of rainfall, while the yield of all other crops varies with the amount of rainfall. The yield of the peanut crop, while constant, is not dominated by any other crop, since some of their yields are higher than, and others lower than, the yield of the peanut crop. See the appendix for the mean and standard deviation of the riskless (certainty) case, or a non-probabilistic distribution.

The Riskiest Case

The riskiest crop is the one with the largest variance (or spread) from minimum to maximum yield and having the worst possible outcome. The worst possible outcome is a zero yield. From table 2.1, there are three crops with a zero yield. Soybeans have the largest variance and a zero yield when rainfall is less than 10 inches, and both grapes and peaches have zero yields when rainfall is greater than 55 inches. As shown in table 2.2, the likelihood of rainfall less than 10 inches is 15 percent, while the likelihood of rainfall greater than 55 inches is 10 percent. Therefore, it is more likely that a rainfall of less than 10 inches will occur than a rainfall greater than 55 inches. This makes soybeans the riskiest crop.

Statistically, risk is defined in terms of the expected value (mean), and the variance, or the square root of the variance, the standard deviation, around the expected value.

The computation of the values in table 2.3 shows that the expected value (or mean) is 31.8 bushels per acre for soybean yield, given the probability distribution for rainfall, R_1 to R_5, and the standard deviation is 37.12 bushels per acre.

The Expected Value (Mean)

The expected value is the sum of the outcomes of an event weighted by the likelihood (or probability) of their occurrence. In the crop example in tables 2.1

Table 2.3
Computation of the Expected Value (Mean), the Variance, and the Standard Deviation for Soybean Crop Yield

Rainfall	Ps	Ys	PsYs	$(Ys - \bar{Y})$	$(Ys - \bar{Y})^2$	$Ps(Ys - \bar{Y})^2$
<10	.15	0	0.0	(31.8)	1011.2	151.7
10–25	.20	15	3.0	(16.8)	282.2	56.4
25–40	.35	35	12.3	3.2	10.2	3.6
40–55	.20	50	10.0	18.2	331.2	66.2
>50	.10	65	6.5	33.2	1102.2	110.2

$$Ys = 31.8 \text{ bushels} \qquad \sigma_s^2 = 1378.1 \text{ bushels}$$

$$\sigma_s = \sqrt{1378.1} = 37.12 \text{ bushels}$$

Source: Tables 2.1 and 2.2

and 2.2, the expected value of the yield of a crop is the yield of the crop for each level of rainfall in table 2.1 weighted by the likelihood of rainfall in table 2.2 as given below:[1]

expected value(s) (of soybean) = (likelihood of R_1) (possible yield for R_1)
+ (likelihood of R_2) (possible yield for R_2)
+ (likelihood of R_3) (possible yield for R_3)   **(2.1a)**
+ (likelihood of R_4) (possible yield for R_4)
+ (likelihood of R_5) (possible yield for R_5).

This relationship can be rewritten in a more compact and symbolic form as follows:

$$\bar{y} = y_1 p_1 + y_2 p_2 + y_3 p_3 + y_4 p_4 + y_5 p_5, \qquad \textbf{(2.1b)}$$

where $\bar{y}$ is the expected value, y_1 is the yield when rainfall is less than 10 inches, y_2 is the yield when rainfall is 10 to 25 inches, y_3 is the yield when rainfall is 25 to 40 inches, y_4 is the yield when rainfall is 40 to 55 inches, y_5 is the yield when rainfall is greater than 55 inches, p_1 is the likelihood of rainfall less than 10 inches, p_2 is the likelihood of rainfall 10 to 25 inches, p_3 is the likelihood of rainfall 25 to 40 inches, p_4 is the likelihood of rainfall 40 to 55 inches, and p_5 is the likelihood of rainfall greater than 55 inches. The expected value (or mean) is the average of the outcomes (yields) weighted by the likelihood of the occurrence of rainfall, the ecological condition necessary to generate the yield of each crop.

Since the expected value (mean) is the weighted average, each outcome (yield) is related to the mean, and it may be either above or below the mean, that is, it is either greater than, less than, or equal to the mean. In other words, the outcomes (yield) are distributed around the mean, and therefore form a distribution.

The Variance

When we have to work with outcomes of an event that varies in a probabilistic way, it is always very useful to know what the mean is and to determine the spread of the outcomes around the mean. This spread is known as the "variance." The variance of a distribution of probabilistic outcomes is the probability-weighted sum of squared deviations from the mean. Using the crop example given in tables 2.1 and 2.2 and the expected value formulated in equations (2.1a) and (2.1b) above, the variance is given as follows:

variance of s = (possible yield for R_1 − expected yield)^2 (likelihood of R_1)
    + (possible yield for R_2 − expected yield)^2 (likelihood of R_2)
    + (possible yield for R_3 − expected yield)^2 (likelihood of R_3)   **(2.2a)**
    + (possible yield for R_4 − expected yield)^2 (likelihood of R_4)
    + (possible yield for R_5 − expected yield)^2 (likelihood of R_5).

The notational form of the variance (σ^2) is

$$\sigma_s^2 = (y_1 - \bar{y})^2 p_1 + (y_2 - \bar{y})^2 p_2 + (y_3 - \bar{y})^2 p_3 + (y_4 - \bar{y})^2 p_4 + (y_5 - \bar{y})^2 p_5, \quad \textbf{(2.2b)}$$

which can be further reduced into compact notational form:

$$\sigma_s^2 = \sum_{i=1}^{5} (y_i - \bar{y})^2 p_i. \quad \textbf{(2.2c)}$$

The Standard Deviation

The standard deviation is another useful statistical tool that standardizes the deviations from the mean and is obtained by taking the square root of the variance. The standard deviation has many important statistical properties that make it of great importance in statistical analysis. The standard deviation of a distribution of probability outcomes is the square root of the probability-weighted sum of squared deviations from the mean. Using equation (2.2b), the standard deviation (σ) is

$$\sigma = [(y_1 - y)^2 p_1 + (y_2 - \bar{y})^2 p_2 + (y_3 - \bar{y})^2 p_3 + (y_4 - \bar{y})^2 p_4 + (y_5 - \bar{y})^2 p_5]^{1/2}. \quad \textbf{(2.3)}$$

In table 2.3, the values of the expected value (mean) [equation (2.1)], the variance [equation (2.2)], and the standard deviation [equation (2.3)], are computed using the data on the crop example in table 2.1 for rainfall and soybean yield and the probability distribution in table 2.2.

The mean and standard deviation can be used to compute additional statistical measures of risk, for example, the coefficient of variation (CV), which gives an index of risk to return. The coefficient of variation is useful because it measures the amount of risk assumed for each bushel (unit) of net yield for the crop example in table 2.1.

When dealing with dollar cash flow, the coefficient of variation measures the amount of risk assumed for each dollar of net cash flow (or for each dollar of return, if returns are being measured). It standardizes the risk per unit of cash flow, and thus makes possible a direct comparison of the risk assumed for each dollar of net cash flow generated by the project.

The CV equals the standard deviation divided by the expected yield of each crop:

$$CV = \frac{\sigma_i}{\bar{y}_i}.$$

Coefficients of variation for the four crops are given in table 2.4. In this example, soybeans have a CV of 1.17, indicating that there is 1.17 units of risk for every unit of yield. This is exceedingly high, and therefore very risky. Recalling that soybeans were selected in the assessment of table 2.1 above as the riskiest crop, the CV corroborates that selection in a more precise way. The higher the CV, the greater the relative riskiness. Peaches have the next highest CV of 0.88 versus a value of 0.48 for grapes, which indicates that the risk assumed per bushel of yield is much greater (1.83 times) for peaches than for grapes. Since there is no variation in the yield for peanuts, the CV is zero, thus making it riskless.

The foregoing discussion and examples of crop yield illustrate the nature of risk, as used in business and investing, and also its measurement. An understand-

Table 2.4
Computation of the Coefficient of Variation for the Crop Example

	Expected Yield $\bar{y}$	Standard Deviation of Yield σ	Coefficient of Variation $\sigma/\bar{y}$
Soybean	31.80	37.12	1.17
Grape	18.15	8.76	0.48
Peanut	20.00	0	0.0
Peach	15.65	13.76	0.88

ing of the nature of risk is a prerequisite for good management, since risk abounds in every area of business management and investing. Once risk is understood and measured, the next step is to investigate how it can be controlled for effective management. The following section deals with the portfolio approach to managing risk.

THE PORTFOLIO APPROACH AND RISK REDUCTION

One approach to risk reduction that is used with great frequency among investors considering opportunities for investment is the diversification of investments among a "portfolio" of assets that have low or negatively correlated cash flows.

Continuing the crop yield example, the portfolio approach is used to combine the various crops in an attempt to reduce the risk inherent in each of the three crops. Recall that of the four crops in table 2.1, only peanuts are riskless, with a constant yield in all the rainfall ranges. It is common knowledge that a farmer will plant a variety of crops to stabilize his income stream. The farmer is unknowingly practicing portfolio strategy. Let us follow the farmer's strategy and combine the three risky crops of soybeans, grapes, and peaches, with one-third the available acreage allotted to each of the three crops. The yield for each crop at each level of rainfall is presented in table 2.5.

In table 2.5, soybean, grape, and peach productions are combined in such a manner that the total output of the combination under each rainfall interval is equal. The total output of the portfolio combination is constant irrespective of the amount of rainfall. The combination ensures an absolutely safe harvest at a higher level of production than produced with peanuts alone.

Note that the portfolio is made up of the three risky crops, and that soybeans, which are so risky that their coefficient of variation is greater than one, are a part

Table 2.5
Portfolio Yield with One-Third Average Allocation for Each of Three Crops

	RAINFALL				
	<10 inches	10-25 inches	25-40 inches	40-55 inches	>55 inches
Soybean	0.0	5.0	12.0	16.7	22.0
Grape	7.0	10.0	6.7	3.3	0.0
Peach	15.0	7.0	3.3	2.0	0.0
Total	22.0	22.0	22.0	22.0	22.0

Source: Table 2.1

of the portfolio. Each of the three crops is risky by itself, but a combination of the three produces a safe harvest.

Table 2.5 illustrates how a portfolio works in reducing risk. When rainfall is less than 10 inches and the soybean crop fails, the grape and peach harvests make up the difference. When rainfall is greater than 55 inches and both the grape and the peach crops fail, the soybean harvest makes up the difference. This indicates that grapes and peaches are negatively correlated with soybeans. When negatively correlated assets are combined, their risks offset each other. In the portfolio combinations shown in table 2.5, grapes and peaches are positively correlated, but negatively correlated with soybeans. The soybean output is roughly equal to the combined output of grapes and peaches at each of the three middle ranges of rainfall. The outputs of grapes and peaches together provide the negative balance to soybeans in constructing the portfolio illustration in table 2.5. Observe that the perfectly negative correlation of the soybean yield enabled us to obtain a portfolio with constant yield at each level of rainfall.

Portfolio Requirement for Risk Reduction

In the portfolio example in table 2.5, the output is constant; there is therefore no variation, and consequently no risk. This example illustrates that by combining perfectly negatively correlated assets, risk can be completely eliminated. Risk can be substantially reduced, though not completely eliminated, in a combination of assets that are less than perfectly negatively correlated. Negative correlation is not a necessary condition for risk reduction: Simple unrelatedness, or independence between the assets, will suffice to achieve some measure of risk reduction. A large number of small unrelated risks will tend to cancel each other out and substantially reduce, if not eliminate, risk.

The principle of continuing unrelated or independent events forms the basis of life insurance. For example, there is a small probability that any individual will die during a year. In normal times, these probabilities are independent; that is, in the absence of a common cause such as a natural disaster, plague, or catastrophic accident, the chance that one individual will die is unrelated to the chance that another individual will die. The number of insurance claims to be paid in any single year can be predicted with a high degree of accuracy, because the number of individuals dying during a year can be accurately predicted. Another example is in banking, where the daily cash needs of each depositor at a bank vary from day to day. If there is independence in the cash needs of different depositors, then the day-to-day variations in each depositor's cash needs will tend to cancel out, making aggregate withdrawals and deposits quite predictable.

MANAGING RISK IN MORTGAGE PORTFOLIOS

Risk in Mortgage Loans

The risk in a mortgage loan arises because of the fluctuations in the net cash flows or in the net income. The fluctuations in the cash inflows result from delinquencies and defaults that interrupt the expected payment stream scheduled when the loan was made. Fluctuations in cash outflows, on the other hand, are due to changes in the administrative overhead cost allocation to the loan. One characteristic common to fluctuations of cash inflows and outflows is the element of uncertainty in (1) whether they will occur and (2) when they will occur. Since there is the uncertainty of their occurrence, there is the possibility that losses may result. It is the probability of losses arising from events that may arise during the life of a loan that may alter the cash flow stream that is at risk. For example, in delinquency, payments are not made when due; the lender loses the use of the funds and the income from their reinvestment. In the case of default, the cash flow from income and repayment of principal is interdicted, with the possibility of loss of both income and principal.

The net cash flow of a loan has a probability distribution that can be described by its mean (or expected value) and the distribution of the fluctuations of the net cash flows around the expected value, which can be measured by its variance or by the standard deviation, which is the square root of the variance.

Risk Profiles and Risk Reduction

Mortgage lenders historically have attempted to minimize risk by developing risk profiles of potentially problem borrowers and rejecting those borrowers who match the profiles during prescreening of loan applicants. Since the risk profiles are developed from past loan performance experience, the presumption is that the pattern experienced in the past will repeat itself. Large numbers of loan applicants are rejected in the process, and the lender is left with a smaller applicant pool after prescreening to make loans. This screening process serves to limit the lender's risk exposure, but, at the same time, it limits the profitability of the lender as well, since premiums for risk can be built into higher rates of interest charged for loans with higher risk. Since the portfolio approach reduces risk, the lender can accept a greater degree of risk from a much larger applicant pool, while minimizing the cost of prescreening.

Risk Reduction in Mortgage Portfolios

The portfolio approach permits the mortgage lender to diversify its lending activities among a "portfolio" of loans that have low or negatively correlated cash flows. Since a variety of events and factors cause delinquency and default in different loans, correlation between the events and factors ranges from high to low, or none at all.

When loans with low or negatively correlated cash flows are incorporated into a portfolio, their combined cash flow will be relatively stable, as shown in the crop example, while generating a desired return. By reducing variability and providing relative stability, the portfolio approach helps reduce risk. The total risk of a portfolio is less than that of the individual assets in the portfolio. A combination of perfectly negatively correlated cash flows will virtually eliminate all the variability in the individual cash flows. As the correlation between the assets increases, portfolio diversification is reduced and its capacity to eliminate risk decreases.

Mortgage Income

The mortgage income to the lender during a period of time is the net interest income (NII), that is, the interest receipt (IR) less the direct interest expense (IE) and the joint common costs of administering the loan portfolio, or overhead (O). The net interest income on a loan can be represented as follows:

net interest income = interest receipt − (interest expense + share of overhead). **(2.4a)**

In notational form, the net interest income is

$$NII = IR - (IE + O). \tag{2.4b}$$

The following example illustrates the calculation of net interest income.

Example 2.1. Assume that a mortgage loan of $1,000 is made for 10 years at 12 percent per annum. The lender pays 9.5 percent per annum for the funds, and the proportional share of overhead cost applicable to the loan is 0.5 percent per annum. Then the net interest income on the loan per year is

$$\begin{aligned} NII &= (\$1,000 \times 0.12) - [(\$1,000 \times 0.095) + (\$1,000 \times 0.005)] \\ &= \$120 - (\$95 + \$5) \\ &= \$20. \end{aligned}$$

To simplify the computation, interest has been computed on an annual basis, in contrast to computation of interest on the monthly balance outstanding, as is done by institutions. The monthly computation yields a slightly higher interest income and a higher effective yield.

For the 10-year life of the loan, the net interest income will be

$$NII = \$20 \times 10 = \$200.$$

This represents the expected actual interest receipts over the life of the loan.

Assigning Probabilities to Cash Flows

At the time the loan is taken out, the mortgage is expected to yield a contractual stream of interest over the life of the loan. The pattern of the stream of interest receipts (or cash inflows) during the life of the loan will be affected by delinquencies and will be significantly altered if default occurs and foreclosure proceedings instituted. Because the pattern of the actual interest receipts is not known with certainty at the time the loan is made, it is considered a random variable with a probability distribution, since the stream of actual interest receipts will vary from the expected stream over the life of the loan. Similarly, the interest cost of the loan principal to the lender will vary with changes in the market rate of interest that affect the cost of deposits. The demise of Regulation Q has significantly increased the impact of market interest rate volatility on deposit rates. It is also expected that overhead costs may change during the life of a long-term mortgage loan. The interest cost and the overhead allocation to the loan make up the cash outflows on the loan.

An estimate of the probable cash flows from the loan under various circumstances such as delinquencies, slow loans, and defaults is then obtained, and an assessment is made of the probability of occurrence of each event. The cash flows for each period are then multiplied by their probabilities and summed to obtain the expected cash flows for each period, which are then discounted by a risk-free discount rate to obtain the present value of the cash flows. The present value of the net cash outflow is subtracted from the present value of the cash inflow to obtain the net present value (NPV).

The uncertainty in the future net cash flows of an asset can be described by a probability frequency distribution when historical data are available. The historical net cash flows are transformed into frequencies and then expressed as probabilities. The probabilities obtained represent the historical return probabilities, which must in turn be adjusted to reflect the expected likelihood of future risks from delinquencies, slow loans, or defaults. The adjusted probabilities are then used as weights to adjust the expected cash flows.

Net Cash Flows

The following examples illustrate the computation of net cash flows and the use of probabilities of loan status occurrence to obtain the expected value of the net cash flow and its associated standard deviation. It is assumed that the cost of funds to the lender is 7.5 percent and that overhead allocation is at 0.5 percent for Mortgage Loan A and Mortgage Loan B.

Example 2.2: Mortgage Loan A. It is assumed that the loan rate is 12 percent, and that if the loan is delinquent, it will be delinquent for about 30 days, or one month. Should default occur, it is assumed that the loan would have been in delinquent/slow status for four months prior to foreclosure action, and a capital gain of $10 would be realized on sale of the foreclosed property.

The net cash flows obtained for Mortgage Loan A in table 2.6 are assigned probabilities reflecting the likelihood of their respective states occurring, shown in table 2.7. The net cash flows and their associated probabilities are used to compute the expected value of the net cash flows and its standard deviation.

The expected value, mean, and standard deviation of Mortgage Loan A's net cash flows are presented in table 2.8. The mean and standard deviation are two measures used to describe the net cash flow and risk relationship of a probability distribution.

Table 2.6
Computation of Net Cash Flow: Mortgage Loan A

Assumptions

Loan rate = 12%; $120 per $1,000	Delinquent = 1 month
Funds rate = 7.5%; $75 per $1,000	Default: 4 months delinquent
Overhead allocation = 0.5%; $5 per $1,000	Capital gain of $10 on sale of property

Net Cash Flow

Loan Status	Cash Inflow	Cash Outflow	Net Cash Flow
Current (good)	$120	$80	$40
Delinquent/slow	110	80	30
Default	90	80	10

The Mean, or Expected, Net Cash Flow

The mean, or expected, net cash flow (C_A) is obtained by summing up the products of the probabilities of occurrence of the three loans' status (S_i) and their net cash flows (C_i). The mean as the probability-weighted average of possible net cash flows computed in table 2.8 can be written as follows:

$$
\begin{aligned}
\text{expected net cash flows} = \ & (\text{probability of } S_1) \ (\text{possible net cash flow for } S_1) \\
& + (\text{probability of } S_2) \ (\text{possible net cash flow for } S_2) \\
& + (\text{probability of } S_3) \ (\text{possible net cash flow for } S_3). \quad \textbf{(2.5a)}
\end{aligned}
$$

Table 2.7
Probability of Loan Status and the Corresponding Net Cash Flows

State of Event (S_A)	Probability of This State of Event Occurring (P_A)	Net Cash Flows if State Occurs (C_A)
Good	.8	$40
Delinquent/Slow	.15	30
Default	.05	10

Table 2.8
Computation of the Expected Net Cash Flow and Standard Deviation for Mortgage Loan A

S_A	P_A	C_A	$P_A C_A$	$(C_A - \bar{C}_A)$	$(C_A - \bar{C}_A)^2$	$P_A(C_A - \bar{C}_A)^2$
Good (S_1)	.8	$40	$32.0	$3	$9	$7.2
Delinq. (S_2)	.15	30	4.5	(7)	49	7.35
Default (S_3)	.05	10	0.5	(27)	729	36.45
			C_A = $37.0			σ_A^2 = $51.00

$$\sigma_A = \sqrt{51} = \$7.14$$

The expected value of the net cash flow (EV [NCF]) can be written in notational forms as

$$\text{EV (NCF)} = P_{S1}C_{A1} + P_{S2}C_{A2} + P_{S3}C_{A3} \qquad (2.5b)$$

or

$$\bar{C}_A = \sum_{i=1}^{3} p_i c_i.$$

In table 2.8, the expected net cash flow from the proposed Mortgage Loan A is $37.00.

The Standard Deviation

The standard deviation provides a measure of the "dispersion" of the possible net cash flows around the mean and thus the riskiness of the loan. First, the deviations from the mean are computed by subtracting the mean from each outcome $(C_A - \bar{C}_A)$ in table 2.8; then those figures are squared. The squared deviations are multiplied by their corresponding probabilities and the products summed to obtain the variance. The standard deviation (σ_A in table 2.8) is written as follows:

standard deviation = [(possible net cash flow for S_1 − expected net cash flow)
(probability of S_1)
+ (possible net cash flow for S_2 − expected net cash flow)
(probability of S_2)
+ (possible net cash flow for S_3 − expected net cash flow)
(probability of S_3)]$^{1/2}$. $\qquad$ (2.6a)

This can be rewritten in notation as

$$\sigma_A = [(C_{A1} - \bar{C}_A)^2 P_S + (C_{A2} - \bar{C}_A)^2 P_{S2} + (C_{A3} - \bar{C}_A)^2 P_{S3}]^{1/2}. \qquad \textbf{(2.6b)}$$

In table 2.8 the computed standard deviation is \$7.14. This figure is used to compare riskiness between mortgage net cash flows.

Example 2.3: Mortgage Loan B. It is assumed that Mortgage Loan B is perceived as a potentially higher risk, and the loan rate is increased by two percentage points to reflect this. Should the loan be delinquent, it will be delinquent for up to 90 days and become a slow loan. There is a higher likelihood of default; and if it occurs, the loan would have been delinquent for about 120 days, or four months, prior to foreclosure action. A capital loss of \$10 would be realized upon sale of the property.

The net cash flows obtained from Mortgage Loan B in table 2.9 are assigned probabilities reflecting the likelihood of their respective states occurring, as shown in table 2.10. The net cash flows and their associated probabilities are used to compute the expected value of the net cash flow and its standard deviation.

In table 2.11, the computed values of the expected net cash flow and the standard deviation for Mortgage Loan B are presented. The expected net cash flow of \$31.65 represents the most likely value of the net cash flow that will be realized from Mortgage Loan B based upon the likelihood probabilities given in table 2.10 and the net cash flows computed in table 2.9 for each loan status.

Table 2.9
Computation of Net Cash Flow: Mortgage Loan B

Assumptions

Loan Rate = 14% = \$140 per \$1000	Delinquent = 3 months
Cost of Funds = 7.5% = \$75 per \$1000	Default: 4 months delinquent
Overhead Allocation = 0.5% = \$5 per \$1000	Capital Loss of \$10 on Sale of Property

Net Cash Flow

Loan Status	Cash Inflow	Cash Outflow	Net Cash Flow
Current (Good)	\$140	\$80	\$60
Delinquent/Slow	105	80	25
Default	70	80	(10)

Table 2.10
Probability of Loan Status and the Corresponding Net Cash Flows

State of Event (S_B)	Probability of This State of Event Occurring (P_B)	Net Cash Flows if state occurs (C_B)
Good	.70	$60
Delinquent/Slow	.15	25
Default	.15	(10)

The expected value of the net cash flows for each period (years) in the life of a loan can be computed with its associated standard deviation as shown for Mortgage Loans A and B. The expected cash flows for the various periods can then be discounted to obtain the percentage value of the net cash flows, which can then be compared with the principal of the loan to be made.

COMPARISON OF THE RISKINESS OF MORTGAGE LOAN A AND MORTGAGE LOAN B

The comparative riskiness of Mortgage Loan A and Mortgage Loan B can be obtained by computing the coefficient of variation for each mortgage from the mean and standard deviation, as was done in the crop example in table 2.4. The CVs for Mortgage Loans A and B are given in table 2.12. Mortgage Loan A has a CV of 0.19 versus that of 0.81 for Mortgage Loan B, which indicates the risk

Table 2.11
Computation of the Expected Net Cash Flow and Standard Deviation for Mortgage Loan B

S_B	P_B	C_B	$P_B C_B$	$(C_B - \overline{C}_B)$	$(C_B - \overline{C}_B)^2$	$P_B(C_B - \overline{C}_B)^2$
Good	.7	$60	42.0	15.75	248.06	173.64
Delinq.	.15	25	3.75	(19.25)	370.56	55.58
Default	.15	(10)	(1.5)	(54.25)	2943.06	441.46
			$\overline{C}_B = \$44.25$			$\sigma_B^2 = \$670.68$

$$\sigma_B = \sqrt{670.68} = \$25.89$$

Table 2.12
Comparison of the Statistics of Mortgage Loan A and Mortgage Loan B

	Expected Net Cash Flow ($\bar{C}$)	Standard Deviation of Net Cash Flow (σ)	Coefficient of Variation (CV)
Mortgage A	$37.00	$7.14	0.19
Mortgage B	31.65	25.89	0.81

assumed for each dollar of net cash flow is much greater in Mortgage Loan B than A. If a choice had to be made between the two mortgage loans on the basis of their relative risk per dollar of expected net cash flow, Mortgage Loan A would be preferred. The standard deviation of Mortgage Loan B (σ_B) is $25.89, which is 3.6 times the standard deviation of Mortgage Loan A, while the expected net cash flow of Mortgage Loan B is 16.9 percent less than the expected net cash flow of Mortgage Loan A, a clear indication that there is relatively more risk in Mortgage Loan B.

THE MORTGAGE PORTFOLIO

Both Mortgage Loan A and Mortgage Loan B are risky investments as shown by their standard deviations and coefficients of variation. Mortgage Loan A is significantly less risky than Mortgage Loan B. To minimize risk, the lender can choose to make Mortgage Loan A only. But is this the only choice available to the lender? Let us recall the crop combination carried out in table 2.5, in which three risky crops were combined to diversify the risks in a portfolio with a stable yield and lower portfolio risk. Using the diversification process, Mortgage Loans A and B can be joined in a way that can reduce their combined risk. Note that the probability of default in Mortgage Loan B is only 15 percent, which indicates that there is a greater likelihood that it may not occur. If it does not occur, the lender stands to gain since the loan interest rate already includes a premium for risk. If the loan defaults in a portfolio combination, Mortgage Loan A would cushion the impact.

Expected Value of Portfolio

The expected net cash flow of a portfolio made up of Mortgage Loan A and Mortgage Loan B, with each loan representing 50 percent of the portfolio, is

$$\bar{C}_p = W_A C_A + W_B C_B, \tag{2.7}$$

where W_A and W_B are the proportions of the portfolio made up of Loans A and B, respectively. Thus,

$$\bar{C}_p = 0.5 \; C_A + 0.5 \; C_B$$
$$= 0.5 \; (\$37) + 0.5 \; (\$31.65)$$
$$= \$34.33.$$

The expected net cash flow of a portfolio made up of 50 percent of Mortgage Loan A and 50 percent of Mortgage Loan B is $34.33, which is $2.67 less than the expected net cash flow of A, but is $2.68 higher than the expected net cash flow of B.

Standard Deviation of Portfolio

The standard deviation of the portfolio is computed with the following formula:

$$\sigma_p = [W_A^2 \sigma_A^2 + W_B^2 \sigma^2 + 2 W_A W_B \; (Cov_{AB})]^{1/2}, \qquad (2.8a)$$

which can be restated as

$$
\begin{matrix}
\text{standard deviation} \\
\text{of the portfolio}
\end{matrix}
=
\left[
\begin{pmatrix} \text{square of} \\ \text{proportion} \\ \text{of A in} \\ \text{portfolio} \end{pmatrix}
\begin{pmatrix} \text{variance of} \\ \text{net cash flows} \\ \text{Mortgage} \\ \text{Loan A} \end{pmatrix}
+
\begin{pmatrix} \text{square of} \\ \text{proportion} \\ \text{of B in} \\ \text{portfolio} \end{pmatrix}
\begin{pmatrix} \text{variance of} \\ \text{net cash flows} \\ \text{in Mortgage} \\ \text{Loan B} \end{pmatrix}
\right.
$$

$$
\left.
+ \; 2
\begin{pmatrix} \text{proportion} \\ \text{of A in} \\ \text{portfolio} \end{pmatrix}
\begin{pmatrix} \text{proportion} \\ \text{of B in} \\ \text{portfolio} \end{pmatrix}
\begin{pmatrix} \text{covariance of net} \\ \text{cash flow A and} \\ \text{net cash flow B} \end{pmatrix}
\right]^{1/2}
\qquad (2.8b)
$$

The Covariance

Cov_{AB} is the covariance of net cash flow A and net cash flow B. The covariance is defined as

$$Cov \; (C_{A1} \; C_B) = \rho_{AB} \sigma_A \sigma_B, \qquad (2.9a)$$

which can be restated as

$$
\begin{matrix}
\text{covariance of net} \\
\text{cash flow A and} \\
\text{net cash flow B}
\end{matrix}
=
\begin{pmatrix} \text{correlation of} \\ \text{net cash flow A} \\ \text{with net cash} \\ \text{flow B} \end{pmatrix}
\begin{pmatrix} \text{standard} \\ \text{deviation} \\ \text{of net cash} \\ \text{flow A} \end{pmatrix}
\begin{pmatrix} \text{standard} \\ \text{deviation} \\ \text{of net cash} \\ \text{flow B} \end{pmatrix}
\qquad (2.9b)
$$

The covariance of the cash flows from the two mortgages is a measure of how their uncertain net cash flows vary together. The correlation coefficient (ρ_{AB})

Table 2.13
Calculation of Covariance of Cash Flows of Mortgage Loan A with Cash Flows of Mortgage Loan B

P_{SA}	$(c_A - \bar{c}_A)$	P_{SB}	$(c_B - \bar{c}_B)$	$P_{SA}(c_A - \bar{c}_A)$	$P_{SB}(c_B - \bar{c}_B)$	$[P_{SA}(c_A - \bar{c}_A)(c_B - \bar{c}_B)P_{SB}]$
.80	3	.70	28.35	2.4	19.84	47.62
.15	(7)	.15	(6.65)	(1.05)	(1.00)	1.05
.05	(27)	.15	(41.65)	(1.35)	(6.25)	8.43
						Cov(c_A c_B) = $57.10

included in equation (2.9a) is a direct measure of the relationship of net cash flow A and net cash flow B. The correlation coefficient can assume a value between -1 and $+1$, where -1 denotes perfect inverse relationship and $+1$ denotes a perfect positive relationship. A negative correlation coefficient implies a negative covariance, which would decrease the portfolio standard deviation. Low correlation has similar effect in reducing the portfolio standard deviation.

A tabular way of computing the covariance is presented in table 2.13. The computations in this table do not contain the correlation coefficient, which may not be readily available in the case of mortgage loans.

Mortgage Portfolio Risk Reduction

Using the variance from table 2.13, the standard deviation is computed as follows:

$$\sigma_p = [(0.25)(51) + (0.25)(670.68) + 2(0.5)(0.5)(57.1)]^{1/2}$$
$$= (12.75 + 167.67 + 28.55)^{1/2}$$
$$= (208.97)^{1/2} = \$14.46.$$

Recall that the standard deviation for Mortgage Loan A was $7.14 and for Mortgage Loan B $25.89. The straight average standard deviation for these two loans would thus be $17.97. But the portfolio standard deviation is only $14.46, a $2.20, or 12.24 percent, reduction from the straight average. Portfolio diversification therefore reduces portfolio risk by reducing the variability in the combined net cash flows. The reduction in portfolio risk comes from three factors: (1) the correlation between the project net cash flows (the lower the correlation less than one, the greater the reduction in risk), (2) the number of mortgage loans in the portfolio, and (3) the proportion or weight of the individual mortgage loans in the portfolio in relation to the correlations among the various loans.

The extent to which the portfolio standard deviation is below a straight average of the standard deviations of Mortgage Loans A and B is directly proportional to how much below one the correlation coefficient is between the loans. The correlation coefficient (ρ_{AB}) is

$$\rho_{AB} = \frac{\text{covariance of net cash flows of Loans A and B}}{(\text{standard deviation of Loan A}) \times (\text{standard deviation of Loan B})}$$

$$= \frac{\text{Cov}\ (C_A,\ C_B)}{AB} \qquad\qquad\qquad \textbf{(2.10)}$$

$$= \frac{57.1}{7.14 \times 25.89}$$

$$= 0.31.$$

The correlation between the cash flows of Mortgage Loans A and B is 0.28. The low correlation has the effect of reducing the portfolio standard deviation below the straight average of the standard deviations. With equal weights given to Loans A and B, the portfolio standard deviation is reduced by 12.24 percent. The portfolio standard deviation can be reduced further if the weights are changed to increase the proportion of the lower-risk loan in the portfolio to 70 percent. The portfolio standard deviation is recomputed to reflect the new weights:

$$\sigma_p = [(0.7)(51) + (0.3)(670.68) + 2(0.7)(0.3)(57.1)]^{1/2}$$
$$= (35.70 + 201.20 + 23.98)^{1/2}$$
$$= (260.88)^{1/2}$$
$$= \$16.15.$$

The new portfolio standard deviation is only \$16.15, which is below the straight average standard deviation of \$17.97. It follows that as the proportion of the loan with the lower standard deviation is increased in the portfolio, the portfolio standard deviation will be reduced and approach the lower standard deviation as its proportion approaches one. The reverse is true when the proportion of Loan B in the portfolio is increased.

EXTENSION OF PORTFOLIO DIVERSIFICATION TO PORTFOLIOS OF MORE THAN TWO MORTGAGE LOANS

Extending this analysis to a portfolio of more than two loans, as the number of loans in the portfolio with low and/or negative covariance is increased up to a point, the portfolio standard deviation will decrease, thus reducing the riskiness of the loan portfolio.

In the preceding analysis, the number of mortgage loans was given; hence, the proportional weights (w_i) were also given. If additional mortgage loans are to be incorporated into the existing portfolio, in order to assess the expected net cash flows and risk effects of each of the new mortgage loan candidates, w_i must be recomputed. This is necessary since the ratio of the investment in a loan to the sum of the investment in the total portfolio obviously changes with the addition of one or more loans. Handling the changes is relatively easy once the portfolio analysis has been programmed into a computer; data on new loans can be easily added, while loans paid up or foreclosed are deleted. The expected cash flow and risk effects can be readily assessed for any number of loans in the portfolio.

CONCLUSION

The preceding analysis indicates that loan managers can reduce risk in the mortgage loan portfolios of their institutions through portfolio diversification. The extent by which the risk is reduced in a portfolio is directly proportional to the correlation coefficient among the project net cash flows and the number of mortgage loans in the portfolio. It has been shown that near maximum reduction in risk can be achieved in a portfolio containing between 10 and 15 loans.

Furthermore, risk reduction through portfolio diversification permits the assumption of mortgage loans with greater variability in their individual net cash flows. Since returns are normally higher for higher risks, the firm can earn higher returns by accepting mortgage loans with higher risks while reducing the risk exposure through portfolio diversification.

NOTE

1. See Appendix 2.A.

APPENDIX 2.A

The mean of a nonprobabilistic distribution, that is, a certain outcome or riskless case, is simply the sum of the outcomes (yields) divided by the number of rainfall ranges:

$$\text{mean (for soybeans)} = \frac{\begin{array}{c}(\text{yield for } R_1 + \text{yield for } R_2 + \text{yield for } R_3 \\ + \text{ yield for } R_4 + \text{yield for } R_5)\end{array}}{\text{number of rainfall ranges}},$$

or in notational form,

$$\bar{y} = \frac{y_1 + y_2 + y_3 + y_4 + y_5}{5}.$$

The variance of a nonprobabilistic distribution, that is, one with certainty, is

$$\text{variance (of soybeans)} = (\text{yield for } R_1 - \text{mean})^2 + (\text{yield for } R_2 - \text{mean})^2 + (\text{yield for } R_3 - \text{mean})^2 + (\text{yield for } R_4 - \text{mean})^2 + (\text{yield for } R_5 - \text{mean})^2,$$

or in notational form,

$$\sigma_s^2 = (y_1 - \bar{y})^2 + (y_2 - \bar{y})^2 + (y_3 - \bar{y})^2 + (y_4 - \bar{y})^2 + (y_5 - \bar{y})^2.$$

This can be restated in compact notation as

$$\sigma_s^2 = \sum_{i=1}^{5} (y_i - \bar{y})^2.$$

The standard deviation is the square root of the variance:

$$\sigma_s = [(y_1 - \bar{y})^2 + (y_2 - \bar{y})^2 + (y_3 - \bar{y})^2 + (y_4 - \bar{y})^2 + (y_5 - \bar{y})^2)]^{1/2}.$$

PART III

Residential Mortgages: Single- and Multifamily

CHAPTER 3

Mortgage Risk Analysis: The Regression Method

This chapter outlines the analytical framework of the regression method used in identifying and measuring those social, economic, and demographic variables seen to be associated with, or contributing to, the risks in mortgage lending.

The technique of regression is suitable for the analysis of mortgage risk for several reasons. First, regression permits the incorporation of qualitative factors that cannot be expressed in quantitative terms, through the use of so-called "dummy variables," into the regression equation.[1] Second, when the dependent variable is scaled as a dummy variable, the regression coefficients that emerge are the same, except for a scale factor, as those that would be yielded by a discriminate function, a second natural choice for this problem.[2] Third, the regression method will yield an index of default or, as it were, an index of loan quality based on borrower and property characteristics. By a suitable extension to be explained in chapter 7, an estimate can be obtained of the probability that a borrower, with given initial personal features as well as property characteristics, will default.

MULTIPLE REGRESSION ANALYSIS

Regression analysis is a statistical method that seeks to explain the variation in a dependent factor, which in this analysis is the quality of the loan, in terms of a number of independent, or "explanatory," factors. The explanatory factors used are the risk factors, which consist of borrower characteristics, property characteristics, loan characteristics, and neighborhood characteristics. A particularly useful feature of the regression method is that it enables the investigator to assess the effect of a given risk factor on loan quality while holding constant and neutralizing the influence of other risk factors.

A regression model may be sketched as follows. If y_t denotes the quality of the tth loan ($t = 1, 2, \ldots, m$) and x_i the ith independent factor ($i = 1, 2, \ldots, n$), it is hypothesized that the loan quality (y_t) consists of the sum of two factors: (1) an explanatory factor, $b_0 + b_1 x_{1t} + b_2 x_{2t} + \ldots + b_n x_{xt}$, where $b_0, b_1, \ldots, b_n$ are said to be the regression coefficients; and (2) an error term, e_t, which can be positive, negative, or zero. The quality of a typical loan can be written as follows:

$$y_t = b_0 + b_1 x_{1t} + b_2 x_{2t} + \ldots + b_n x_{nt} + e_t.$$

For a typical loan, its associated borrower, property, loan, neighborhood, and lender characteristics (the x_i's) can be multiplied by each of its associated risk coefficients (the b_i's) and these products summed to obtain the explanatory factor. For example, suppose there is but one risk factor, x_1, and that $b_0 = 0.01$ while $b_1 = 0.09$. If, for a given loan, $x_1 = 1$, then the explanatory factor for this loan would be $0.01 + (0.09)1 = 0.1$. The error term, e_t, denotes the deviation of the explanatory factor, 0.1, from the actual quality of this loan, y_t. Over all loans, e_t is assumed to have a frequency distribution with an expected value of zero.

The values of the coefficients $b_0, b_1, \ldots, b_n$ must be estimated from sample data. Using such data, standard least-squares procedures enable one to estimate these coefficients. These sample estimates of the corresponding coefficients are denoted as $b_0, b_1, \ldots, b_n$, and hence the predicted quality of a loan as

$$y_t = b_0 + b_1 x_{1t} + b_2 x_{2t} + \ldots + b_n x_{nt}.$$

Two statistical measures are frequently highlighted in regression studies. The first measure is the coefficient of determination or the R^2, the square of the correlation coefficient. The larger this quantity is, the greater is the proportion of the variation in loan quality that is "explained" or "accounted for" by the explanatory factor. While the existence of correlation does not necessarily imply causation, if there is cause and effect, then there must be correlation.

A second measure of importance is the test of significance that is applied to each regression coefficient, a measure that enables one to make allowances for sampling error in assessing the magnitude of a variable's associated regression coefficient. If a coefficient is deemed significant, which is a way of saying that its magnitude relative to its standard error is too large to be attributed to mere chance, then the associated variable is considered a useful explanatory variable.

THE EXPLANATORY FACTORS

A discussion of the explanatory factors that can be used in a regression model to analyze mortgage risk is presented under four general categories: (1) risk factors associated with the loan itself, (2) risk factors associated with the borrower, (3) risk factors associated with the property, and (4) risk factors associated with the location of the property, the neighborhood.

Loan Characteristics

The *loan-to-value ratio* is an indicator of the magnitude of the loan on the borrowing date relative to the purchase price of the property. This ratio is considered to be one of the most important variables in a study of mortgage risks. The size of the mortgage loan relative to the value of the house determines the amount of equity of the mortgagor. The higher the loan-to-value ratio, the lower will be the amount of the owner's equity and, for any given term to maturity, the higher will be the monthly payment-to-income ratio. The higher payment-to-income ratio increases the financial burden of the mortgagor, which may accelerate the pressure on the mortgagor to become delinquent when contingencies arise. If the pressure is of sufficient magnitude and duration, the borrower may end up defaulting on the loan. For any given term to maturity, as the loan-to-value ratio approaches one, the loan quality may deteriorate in an accelerative manner.

For residential mortgages, lenders normally divide the L/V ratio into three or more ranges: less than 85 percent, 85 to 90 percent, and over 90 percent.

The *term to maturity* is the duration of the loan from the date the loan is executed. A longer term to maturity allows repayment of the loan to be stretched out over a longer period of time, increasing the time exposure of the lender. The longer term to maturity permits smaller monthly installment payments and lowers the monthly payment-to-income ratio, thereby reducing the riskiness of the loan. The opposing risk effects of these two factors create some uncertainty as to whether risk is increased or decreased with the lengthening of the term to maturity. The direction of change in the riskiness of the loan will appear to depend upon the net effect of the two countervailing risk forces. If the reduction in risk from a lower payment-to-income ratio is greater than the increased time exposure of the lender, then lengthening the term to maturity decreases the riskiness of the loan. The lower payment-to-income ratio provides increased financial flexibility for the borrower to meet future contingencies, thereby reducing the possibility of interruption in repayment of the mortgage. The reduction in risk that results from the borrower's increased financial capacity to meet contingencies is believed to be of greater magnitude than any increment in risk due to the lender's increased time exposure as a result of a lengthening of the term to maturity.

The *total payment-to-income* ratio is an important variable because it measures the mortgagor's financial capacity. Total payment is made up of the borrower's monthly mortgage payment of principal and interest plus property taxes and insurance premiums. This ratio relates total payment obligation under the mortgage loan to the borrower's monthly income at the time the loan is executed. This variable can be broken up into classes to examine the effect of PITI on various ranges of income, such as over 30 percent, 23 to 29 percent, and under 23 percent. If taxes and insurance are not escrowed by the lending institution, the ratio may be taken as simply the ratio of the mortgage payment (principal and interest) to monthly income. When this is done, it is important to account elsewhere for the borrower's ability to meet tax and insurance payments.

The lower the total payment-to-income ratio, the greater is the borrower's capacity to meet the financial obligations of the loan and also meet contingencies and other sporadic financial problems that may arise. The converse is that as this ratio rises, the borrower's financial viability is measurably reduced, increasing the risks of delinquency as unexpected contingencies arise and possible default if the problem perserveres. This factor also measures the financial burden that the borrower is carrying; and it is believed that the higher this ratio, the less able a borrower is to weather financial stress and, all other things given, the lower will be the quality of the loan. This factor is therefore positively correlated with mortgage risk.

The *purpose of the mortgage loan* distinguishes between loans for purchase and for refinancing. This factor is important because it describes the nature of the transaction and identifies the need to be met, as well as the type of risk exposure that the lender is undertaking.

1. A loan to purchase is a new commitment in which both parties, the borrower and the lender, enter into a contract after a full-scale determination and screening of the borrower's ability to meet the loan obligations. It is generally the case that when a borrower applies for a mortgage to purchase a residence, there will not be any other debt obligation of that magnitude that will impair the borrower's ability to meet the loan obligations satisfactorily. In the screening process, the lender is in a position to accept or reject: (1) the application of the borrower, (2) the property to be mortgaged in support of the loan. The lender (mortgagee) sets out the minimum standards that the borrower should meet for the loan to be granted. Accordingly, the lender is in full control of the situation and enters the contract with full realization of the borrower's status and capacity. The lending institution can specify also the proportion of the cost of the property that will be financed through the loan, the L/V ratio, thus minimizing its risk exposure by asking for a higher down payment and thereby increasing the equity shield contribution of the borrower. In the case of purchase, the lender is in a position to control to varying degrees the risk exposure in the loan to be made.

If the need for refinancing should arise during the life of a loan because the borrower is experiencing difficulties with the mortgage, greater risk would be expected with such a loan than with new financing. While the difference in these qualities may be significant, one would not expect it to be markedly significant.

2. There are two general refinancing cases. The first case is refinancing a first mortgage loan because the borrower wants to lower the mortgage interest rate below the existing rate in the mortgage. The second case is when the borrower takes out a second mortgage for some specific need. The treatment of the first case of refinancing a first mortgage loan is the same as the treatment in purchase.

Loans to refinance a second mortgage consist of the provision of additional funds beyond the first mortgage by the lender to the borrower.[3] The borrower needs the funds to meet some specific purpose such as maintenance, repairs, renovation, or extension of the property or for needs not related to the mortgaged property. The additional loan on the property is usually covered by the equity built up by the mortgagor in the mortgaged property through the years, and the borrower has been in good credit standing and has demonstrated the ability to meet the mortgage commitments. Such a proven record should, under normal circumstances, indicate a lower risk problem in this kind of a loan. The size of the installment payments are increased, and the larger payments may result in reducing the borrower's ability to weather any financial problems in the future, thereby increasing the risk exposure. It is not difficult to conceive how the existence of a second mortgage refinancing loan may lead to delinquency or foreclosure, should financial adversity befall the mortgagor.

Conventional, FHA, or VA mortgage is a classification that reflects the type of financing. Conventional mortgages are the norm, but frequently borrowers turn to FHA or VA financing primarily because they fail to meet conventional mortgage criteria. FHA or VA mortgages would therefore be riskier than conventional mortgages. VA mortgages would in turn be riskier than FHA loans because of the extremely high loan-to-value ratios allowed.

Borrower Characteristics

The *occupation* of the borrower reflects the type of employment or business in which the borrower is engaged. Certain types of occupations are considered riskier than others because of their relative instability in terms of tenure, income, or mobility. New, and small, businesspersons as well as unskilled labor are perceived as being somewhat unstable in tenure, which may result in loss of earning power. Similarly, unskilled labor is subject to the vicissitudes of conditions, and salesmen are well known for their sudden changes in fortune. Some employment categories such as executive and middle management suffer from frequent or periodic transfers from one place to another. In other cases, the incidence of layoff periods would indicate the possibility of periodic loss of income. The biennial or triennial strikes of skilled workers and clerical workers in unions are periods of temporary loss of income.

The stability of income in each category of employment can best be portrayed in a relative sense by comparing one category with another. Tenure of employment can also be treated in a comparative way to show relative riskiness. For statistical analysis, the employment categories would be treated in a qualitative way, or as dummy variables. In comparative analysis, it is most convenient to use one category as the point of reference, the base category. Any category can be employed as the base category, but in measuring the relative riskiness of the occupation classes, a useful procedure is to set the most stable occupation as the base category. The executive category could be considered the most stable occupation and used as the base category for comparing the other categories. The general employment categories are executive, middle management and supervisory, professional, own business, building trades, salesman, clerical, teacher or professor, arts, skilled labor, unskilled labor, farm, military, government, manufacturer's representative, and pensioned.[4]

In some instances, a borrower may fall into several categories. The borrower should be placed into the occupational category that provides the principal source of income. An unskilled worker employed by a governmental employer would be classified as government.

Years employed with current employer is intended to represent the number of years the borrower has been employed with his current employer as of the date of the mortgage. The longer a borrower has been employed with his current employer, the more stable are the income prospects, unless he is close to retirement or the employer goes out of business. Hence, it is conjectured that this factor may be a proxy for borrower income stability. The risk of loss resulting from income instability would be expected to decrease as the number of years the borrower was employed in his current employment increased.

The *age of borrower* on the date the mortgage is executed is also treated as a qualitative, or dummy, variable, by breaking it into age groups to examine their relative riskiness. The age groups are under 30, between 30 and 50, and over 50 for inclusion in the regression analysis.

Up to a certain age bracket, family income increases with age. Also, more responsible and disciplined payment habits may be associated with more mature age groups. Finally, mature people have had more experience in handling family budgets and in anticipating as well as confronting personal financial crises. For these reasons, one might predict loan quality increasing with age, at least to a certain extent, until health problems and limited reemployment opportunities begin to plague workers in older age groups.

The *number of children* in the family of the borrower on the date of the mortgage is perceived to be an explanatory factor of loan quality. All other things given, the greater the number of children, the greater the financial obligations of a borrower. Loan quality may diminish as the number of children in the borrower's family increases.

Property Characteristics

The *price of property* refers to the price of the property on the date of the mortgage. This price should be adjusted by the local consumer price index to remove the inflationary factor.

Purchasers of higher-priced property are presumed to be better risks than purchasers of lower-priced property, on the assumption that they have significantly higher net worths. Since it may be very difficult to obtain consistent, reasonably accurate estimates of borrower net worth, the price of property may serve to some degree as a proxy for the borrower's overall net worth.

The *age of property* factor represents the chronological age of the building or structure on the mortgaged property on the date of the mortgage. It is reasonable to suppose that buyers of older, nonmodernized physical structures in decaying neighborhoods would have less incentive to make the heavy expenditures necessary to substantially lengthen the useful life of such structures. The value of the land in such cases could, in time, be greater than the value of the structure. When this happens, the mortgagor may wish to sell, and if buyers cannot be found, the mortgagor may be inclined to abandon the structure in default. It follows that one would expect increases, rather than decreases, over time in the loan-to-loan-value ratios of such mortgages as the value of the structure declined, thereby reducing the incentive of the borrower to repay the loan.

Neighborhood Characteristics

The *median per capita income* is the level of per capita income in the last census in the community or neighborhood. The change in per capita income between the last two censuses, or the percentage change in median per capita income for the same period, may also be used in the analysis to reflect the changes in the neighborhood income profile.

This neighborhood factor should have a beneficial effect on loan quality. The higher the level, or change, in income, the greater the financial capacity of property owners in a community to sustain adversity and maintain, or enhance, property values, providing a favorable effect on the property value of a given mortgage. Rising property values result in declining loan-to-value ratios, thereby increasing loan quality.

The *population* factor represents the number of people residing in the municipality in which the property is located at the last census. The change in population between the last two censuses may also be incorporated in the analysis.[5] The percentage change may be used in place of the change itself.

It is difficult to conjecture the effect of this factor on loan quality. It is suspected that its effect depends on the level or density of the attained population in the community as well as other community factors such as average age of structures. For example, in newly developing and burgeoning neighborhoods in sections of the city, and more likely located in the suburbs, property values are likely to increase with population growth, thus lowering the loan-to-value ratio. Hence, the risk of mortgages in such communities can be expected to decline with population growth. On the other hand, when population density reaches a critical level, older housing is able to sustain particularly heavy use by large numbers of children, but continued increases in population are likely to produce greater risk, if unaccompanied by increased ability to pay.

The *crime rate* effect is another relationship over which there is little disagreement. The higher the crime rate, the greater the downward pressure on property values, nudging upward loan-to-value ratios and hence the prediction of a declining loan quality for loans in such communities. Reported crime is presumably understated in some areas relative to others, and it may be that areas in which

Table 3.1
List of Factors and Hypothesized Direction of Change. Predicted Risk Effect of Factors

A factor with a plus sign denotes that default or delinquency factor risk is expected to increase with increases in the explanatory. A minus sign indicates inverse relationship.

Explanatory Factors	Sign
Loan Property and Borrower	
Loan-to Loan-Value[1]	+
Payment-to-Income	+
Price of Property	−
Term to Maturity (years)	−
Age of Property[2]	+
Years employed in current occupation[3]	−
Age of Borrower (30 - 50)	−
(over 50)	+
(under 30)	+
Number of Children	+
New Financing	−
FHA	+
VA	+
Conventional	−

people are particularly good risks in mortgage lending report a higher percentage of crimes committed. If true, this might mask the relationship between levels of crime and mortgage risk.

Crime data are classified on the basis of personal crimes and property crimes. Personal crimes are those crimes against a person, and property crimes are crimes against property. The number of occurrences of each type of crime is expressed as rate per 1,000 population.

It is difficult to determine the effect of the *unemployment rate* on loan quality from the problems that exist in the definition of work force participants, es-

Table 3.1 (*Continued*)

Explanatory Factors	Sign
Neighborhood	
Change in income – prior census – Last census	–
Change in population – Prior census – Last census[4]	–
Crime rate – personal	+
Crime rate – property	+
Unemployment rate	+
Level of income – Last census	–
Level of population – Last census[4]	–
Percent change in income – Prior census to last census	–
Percent change in population – Prior census to last census[4]	–

[1]Particularly over 90 percent.

[2]If the property is not well maintained, may have a strong positive trend.

[3]Unless where mortgagor is old or the company is in precarious financial condition.

[4]An increase in population in a growing or stable neighborhood decreases risk. In a deteriorating neighborhood may very well increase risk.

pecially in applying this definition over a span of time. Temporary unemployment is perceived to be an important explanatory variable for delinquency risk. Protracted structural unemployment among the possible mortgagors in a community, on the other hand, could induce reduced property maintenance and abandonment of some houses in the neighborhood, depress loan-to-value ratios, and encourage some borrowers to default. Data on this statistic may be more difficult to obtain. Structural unemployment is presumably closely correlated with the overall unemployment rate, and as such loan quality in a given community ought to decline with increases in the unemployment rate.

All the hypotheses discussed above about the risk effects of the explanatory factors are summarized in table 3.1. The signs suggest the expected effect of an explanatory factor on loan quality after the effects of all other factors have been removed.

A dichotomized dependent variable should be used in the regression analysis: for foreclosure risk, between accounts that are foreclosed and those that are currently "good"; and for delinquency risk, between accounts that are delinquent and those that are good. If there is interest to compare delinquency and foreclosure risks, then the dependent variable should be dichotomized between accounts that are delinquent and those that are foreclosed.

EXCLUDED FACTORS

It may not be possible to include all elements that have an ex ante influence on loan quality. Either data on a number of variables may not be available or it would be prohibitively costly to obtain them. These factors, however, may be expected to have only a slight or second-order influence on loan quality, at best. Nevertheless, to mitigate, or soften, the influence these excluded factors may have on the analysis, the data-sampling procedure should provide for randomization over these influences. Where sampling is not possible owing to the paucity of mortgages in an institution, the analysis should include the entire frame of mortgages.

NOTES

1. Examples of qualitative variables are race, sex, and occupation.
2. See chapter 6.
3. Most refinancing takes the form of a second mortgage loan on the property. During high rates of inflation, real estate values appreciate rapidly, building up owner's equity, and second mortgage refinancing becomes very attractive and convenient for both lenders and borrowers. Lenders use the buildup of owner's equity as collateral for loans to the borrower.
4. These are general classifications only and can be subclassified; for example, salesman: insurance, real estate, etc. Also, computer operators can be either professional or clerical.
5. The Census Bureau also takes a mid-decade census from a scientific sample that gives a fair idea of the changes taking place before the next complete census is taken.

APPENDIX 3.A. ANALYTICAL BIASES AND CONSTRAINTS OF THE DATA

A marked bias in the data resulted from data misclassification. While it was always possible to determine the accounts currently delinquent, in many savings and loan associations, it was not possible to find out if a current or delinquent account had been delinquent in the past.

The result is that current good accounts can include a substantial proportion of formerly delinquent accounts that should be classified as delinquent for analytical purposes. This makes it more difficult to obtain statistically significant results and identify risk factors.

Another restriction on the scope of the analysis pertains to the date of reference of borrower, loan, and property information. Only information on those items that were available at the time the loan was executed and available to the associations' loan committees was employed in the study. Changes in borrower, loan, and property features occurring after the date of the loan were not included as explanatory variables. We were restricted in our study to the use of readily available data. The cost of follow-up to each borrower (current, delinquent, and foreclosed) would have been substantially beyond the financial scope of this study and the time allowed for its completion. We ruled out, fairly early in the project, any prospect of predicting risk of marital breakup or of housing values. We focused on utilizing information generally available to lenders:

1. Loan application
2. Appraisal reports
3. Census information
4. Police department reports.

A constraint with possible adverse statistical implications involved limitations on the quantity and quality of the data, as well as semantic obstacles. Among savings and loan associations, definitions of even commonly understood concepts are not uniform. Some collect certain bits of information that others do not. Some retain information only on active files, otherwise they are destroyed. Mortgage files may or may not contain information on past delinquent accounts. Reports for earlier periods may have been destroyed. All of these factors should be adjusted for, either through direct data adjustments or through eliminating certain mortgages because of lack of comparability, which thereby would obviously reduce the ultimate sample size.

To quantitatively determine the effect of one or more variables on another, it is essential to have as much variation as possible in these so-called "explanatory" factors. Preselection criteria, by their very operation, reduce the variance in the explanatory factors, making the task of explaining variation in mortgage performance more difficult, or, putting it in still another way, limiting the discriminating ability of these factors to distinguish good from bad in mortgage performance. The data usually available, by necessity, are preselected data of individuals who were accepted by the lender to have mortgages. Those persons who failed to meet the lender's minimal selection criteria would have been rejected and the data may not be available. This fact introduces a bias in the data, which unfortunately cannot be corrected, discounted, or allowed for in the quantitative results; it also diminishes markedly the ability of the statistical methods to identify, measure, and assess risk factors in mortgage lending, thereby making it less likely that some factors that are in fact significant and important will manifest themselves.

The significance of this may be highlighted through an example. Suppose a lender were to choose for mortgage lending only persons with annual incomes of $22,000. The effect of income on default risk could not be ascertained if there were no variation in income data. As another example, if an association rejected all applicants with certain combinations of levels of some variables, the default effect of these could not be known if they were not even permitted to exist.

REFERENCES

Anderson, T. W. *Introduction to Multivariate Statistical Analysis*. New York: John Wiley & Sons, 1958.

Fryer, H. C. *Concepts and Methods of Experimental Statistics*. Boston: Allyn & Bacon, 1964.

Goldberger, A. S. *Econometric Theory*. New York: John Wiley & Sons, 1964.

Huang, David S. *Regression and Econometric Methods*. New York: John Wiley & Sons, 1970.

Johnston, J. *Econometric Methods*. New York: McGraw-Hill, 1972.

CHAPTER 4

Linear Probability Model

This chapter presents the linear probability regression model, which is used to analyze both default and delinquency risks.[1] The regression results will indicate which factors have significant influences on risk independently of the peculiarities of the lending institution.

The other aspects of the borrower that may be important indicators of default and delinquency risks are not included in the regression analyses because they cannot be measured. These include family characteristics such as personality, marital happiness or strife, and incidence of divorce. Some of these types of attributes may be known to the lending officer, but are usually not recorded on an application.

THE LINEAR PROBABILITY MODEL

The linear probability model, as its name implies, gives the probability of the occurrence of the risk that is being analyzed.[2] The loan officer can then use the probability obtained to determine whether or not to make the loan.

The linear probability model is one type of the general regression form, in which the dependent factor is assigned either a value of zero or a value of one.[3] For example, in comparing foreclosed loans with good loans, the foreclosures are given a value of one and good loans are given a value of zero.[4] Thus, the value of one is always given to loans in the poorest performance category.

This method of coding the dependent variable will affect the signs of the computed regression coefficients. Because inferior-performing loans are assigned a value of 1, independent factors tending to decrease loan quality will have positive signs, while those tending to increase quality will have negative signs. Viewed in another way, a factor with a positive coefficient tends to increase the risk of a loan; a factor with a negative coefficient decreases the risk of a loan. For example, one may assume that as the loan-to-value ratio increases, a loan becomes more risky. If this assumption is correct, then in the regression equations, the "loan-to-value" (or loan-to-price) variable should have a positive coefficient, indicating that an increase in the loan-to-value ratio increases the riskiness of a loan. If the problem of testing whether or not a specific regression coefficient is significantly different from zero is ignored for the moment, it can be said that a negative coefficient implies that an increase in the associated variable will decrease risk, while a positive coefficient implies that an increase in the associated variable will increase the risk.

In order to isolate the specific effects of the risk being analyzed, when foreclosed loans are compared with good loans, all delinquent loans are deleted from the sample. Similarly, when delinquent loans are compared with good loans, all foreclosed loans are deleted from the sample. Every loan is thus classified as either foreclosed, delinquent, or good.[5]

The regression equations of the linear probability model estimated compared foreclosed loans with good loans and delinquent loans with good loans using various combinations of explanatory variables. The regression results presented in this chapter were selected on the basis of several significant characteristics: first, the overall significance of the equation as measured by the F statistic; second, the value of R^2; and third, the signs, magnitudes, and statistical significance of the individual regression coefficients.

Correlation Among the Explanatory Factors

Explanatory factors usually bear some relationship with each other in varying degrees. The interrelationships among the independent factors cause them to covary together. The degree to which two factors are related to each other is measured by the correlation coefficient, with values of -1 to $+1$. Two factors very highly correlated with each other will have a correlation coefficient (r_{yx}) equal to $+1$ when they are positively correlated and equal to -1 when they are negatively correlated. All other correlations fall within this interval.

The simple correlation, r_{yx}, indicates the relationship between each explanatory factor, x, and the dependent factor, y. The correlation coefficient indicates whether or not above-average values of the dependent factor tend to occur with above-average values of the explanatory factors. The correlation coefficient does not take into account the influence of other factors in the equation, while the regression coefficient does.

A correlation matrix should be constructed to determine the degree of relationship among the explanatory factors. If two factors that are highly correlated with each other are included in the regression equation, one of the factors will not be significant. That is, its explanatory power will be very minimal, because the other factor has explained away the relationship with the dependent factor. Highly correlated variables must be separated and those factors with less explanatory power dropped from the equation. Correlated variables are said not to be statistically independent of each other.

There are various ways of removing highly correlated factors. One way is on the basis of theoretical relationship, which identifies the factors with the strongest a priori relationships. An alternative approach is to include all the factors and then remove correlated factors that are not significant. A third way is through stepwise regression, by including the factors one at a time. A fourth is to regress different combinations of factors.

Factors shown to have high correlation coefficients, for example, 0.60 to 1.00, are known a priori not to have great explanatory power and can be removed. There are other factors with correlation coefficients between 0.40 and 0.60 that can be removed if they are known to have low explanatory power. Otherwise they can be included in different combinations to see how they perform. Sometimes, a variable that is not significant in one combination may become much more significant in another.

TREATMENT OF QUALITATIVE FACTORS

A qualitative factor, or dummy variable, is a nonquantifiable discontinuous variable that takes the value of one or zero depending on whether or not the loan being studied possesses a certain characteristic.

Qualitative variables are included in the regression analysis to indicate whether the loan is conventional, FHA, or VA. Other qualitative variables are used to indicate whether the loan is refinanced, whether there is junior financing, whether the loan has private insurance coverage, and the type of property, for example, single- or multifamily dwelling. The following values were given the qualitative factors:

FHA	: 1,	not FHA	: 0,
VA	: 1,	not VA	: 0,
refinanced	: 1,	not refinanced	: 0,
junior financing	: 1,	not junior financing	: 0,
multifamily dwelling	: 1,	single dwelling	: 0,
private insurance	: 1,	other insurance or not private insurance	: 0.

The importance of the treatment here is to identify the effect of the factors that take on the value of one on the riskiness of the loan. The assigned value of one gives these factors a positive value, and their coefficients will be positive. This implies that their presence increases the riskiness of the loan.

Occupational factors representing a number of occupational classes are treated as qualitative factors, or dummy variables, to determine the relative effects of the different classes on default risk. Suppose an occupational factor contains N classes; then $(N - 1)$ factors are used in the equation to represent the N occupational classes in addition to a constant term. For example, in this analysis, each borrower is classified by occupation into one of six different occupational groups as shown in table 4.2 (p. 67). One of these groups—professional, skilled labor, and building tradesmen—is chosen as the base group. The remaining five groups then become five new dummy variables. If a borrower belongs to the category of middle management, then variable 1 is assigned a value of 1 and the other five variables representing the five other groups are each given a value of zero. Alternatively, if a person is a farmer, then variable 5 is given the value of 1 and the other five variables are given the value of zero.

The coefficient of any particular variable measures the change in the influence or effect of that variable on the dependent variable, owing to its being in a particular category as opposed to being in the base category. A positive coefficient indicates that the particular category is riskier than the base category. A negative coefficient indicates that the particular category is less risky than the base category.

Nonlinear Factors

Other qualitative factors are also treated for their nonlinear effects on default risk. These qualitative factors include (1) the age of the mortgagor, (2) the loan-to-value ratio, and (3) the ratio of monthly payment to monthly income.[6]

The *age of mortgagor* factor is believed to have differential effects on default risk within different age groups. The age factor is divided into three age groups to capture their separate differential effects. These effects are expected to indicate just how risky each group is relative to the other groups. For example, it is known that young adults up to age 30 are at the beginning of their career and in the process of family formation or family building. This group has limited financial resources with growing family responsibilities. Those in the 30 to 50 age group, on the other hand, are in the prime of their careers, with high income and heavy family responsibilities during the period when the children are in college. Persons in the 50 and over age group are generally in the upper levels of their careers, with very high incomes and most or all of the children graduated from college, leaving high levels of discretionary income available for retirement planning.

The age variable is divided into the following three age groups: less than 30 years, 30 to 50 years, and over 50 years. To make comparisons, one age group is used as the base group. Since persons in the 30 to 50 age group are at the prime of their careers, with family formation in place, this group is assumed the least risky and logically represents the base category for comparative purposes. Each of the two other age groups, under 30 and over 50 years, is each compared with the base group of 30 to 50 years. The age of each borrower for each loan is classified as a variable as follows:

less than 30 years : 1, otherwise : 0,
over 50 years   : 1, otherwise : 0.

The base age group, 30 to 50 years, carries a value of zero. The two age groups being compared with the base group will be riskier, or less risky, than the base group by comparison.

Different ranges of the *loan-to-value ratio* have differential effects on default risk. This can easily be gleaned from the reciprocal of the loan-to-value ratio, the equity-to-value (E/V) ratio. The greater the initial equity invested by the borrower in the property, the higher the borrower's stake and the lower the risk that the borrower will default or abandon the property. Lenders usually delineate the L/V ratio into intervals: less than 85 percent, 85 to 90 percent, and over 90 percent. The higher the initial equity, the lower the loan amount, which makes the less than 85 percent L/V ratio the least risky and the logical base category. The other two categories, 85 to 90 and over 90 percent, will be compared with the base category to examine their effects on default risk, and the following values were given to the two qualitative L/V factors:

> L/V ratio over 90 percent   : 1, otherwise : 0,
> L/V ratio 85 to 90 percent : 1, otherwise : 0.

The base category, L/V ratio less than 85 percent, is given the value of zero. The two other categories will have positive coefficients, indicating that they are riskier than the base category.

Payment-to-income ratio represents the monthly payment to monthly income of the mortgagor. When the monthly payment makes up a very small proportion of the monthly income, the mortgagor is able to make the monthly mortgage payment without any difficulty and has enough income left over to meet the family obligations. As the amount of the monthly payment increases relative to the amount of the monthly income, a higher proportion of the income is needed to meet the mortgage payment, and a correspondingly smaller proportion of the monthly income is available to meet the family needs. The greater the financial constraint, the higher the chances that any financial problems will result in default. The payment-to-income ratio is divided into three intervals to reflect lenders' perceived risk patterns: less than 22 percent, 22 to 30 percent, and over 30 percent. Since the lower the payment-to-income ratio, the lower the risk, the less than 22 percent group is assumed to have the lowest risk and is used as the base category for comparison with the other two risk classes. The two other risk classes are given the following values:

> P/I ratio over 30 percent   : 1, otherwise : 0,
> P/I ratio 22 to 30 percent : 1, otherwise : 0.

It is important to note that for each set of dummy variables, one category must be chosen as the base with which the other categories are compared. It is especially important to note which category has been chosen as the base because each of the dummy variable coefficients measures the effect of being in a specific category as opposed to being in the base category.

STATISTICAL MEASURES OF THE EXPLANATORY
POWER OF THE REGRESSIONS

The statistical measures that are used to measure the explanatory power of a regression equation are the coefficient of determination (R^2), the standard error, and the F statistic.

Multivariate regression is aimed at explaining the overall variation in the dependent factor by using various explanatory (or independent) factors. The value of R^2 serves as a useful measure of how well the explanatory factors account for the total variation in loan quality, the dependent factor. It measures the percentage of the variation in the dependent factor that is explained by the independent variables. Provided the regression equation contains a constant term, the value of R^2 will always be between zero and one. High values of R^2 indicate a good-fitting equation; that is, the use of the independent factors accounts for a large percentage of the variation in loan quality.

The F ratio gives an indication of the explanatory power of the factor in assessing the degree of risk. If the F statistic is significantly different from zero, the explanatory variables account for more of the variation of the dependent variable than could be attributed to chance. To determine if the F statistic is significantly different from zero, first select some level of significance, for example, 95 percent; then, using the tabulated values, find the critical value F. If the calculated value is greater than the critical value F, this indicates that the F value is significantly different from zero at the 95 percent level of significance. Thus, high values of the F statistic are interpreted as meaning that the explanatory power of the factor is not due to chance.

An F statistic can also be computed for the regression equation as a whole. As the number of explanatory factors in the equation is increased, a higher proportion of the variation of the dependent factor can be accounted for. The critical value F depends on the number of factors in the equation, the number of observations, and the desired level of significance. The overall F statistic is a nonlinear transformation of the value of R^2 and is used to test the overall significance of the regression equation.

The size of a factor's coefficient indicates its relative explanatory power. The larger the coefficient, the greater its explanatory power. In a comparison of two explanatory factors, the factor with the larger coefficient has more explanatory power than the factor with the smaller coefficient.

EMPIRICAL RESULTS: DEFAULT RISK

The regression results for default risk are presented in table 4.1.[7] The table shows the factors, the values of the coefficients obtained from the regression analysis, and their F ratios. The R^2 and the overall F ratio for this regression are 0.089 and 4.793, respectively.[8]

The L/V ratio is shown to be an important factor in default analysis. As discussed in the treatment of explanatory factors, the L/V ratio is divided into three intervals to detect nonlinear effects. The coefficient of the L/V interval of

Table 4.1
Coefficients and *F* Ratios of Explanatory Variables in Default Risk**

Variable	Coefficient	F Ratio
Loan to loan value:		
Over 90%	0.08235*	16.75
85 - 90%	0.04421	2.46
Payment to income:		
Over 30%	0.09180*	7.80
22 - 30%	-0.02703	1.49
Age of mortgagor:		
Over 50	0.04465*	3.24
Less than 30	-0.02609	2.32
Number of years with employer	-0.00367*	15.76
Age of property	0.00049	1.57
Junior financing	0.19653*	13.75
Unemployment rate	0.60069*	4.50
Per capita changes in crimes against property	-0.34399	0.34
VA insurance	0.00128	0.00
FHA insurance	-0.09032*	12.26
Price of property	-0.00279*	15.52
Number of children	0.00695	2.38
Refinanced loan	0.06178*	4.55
Term of loan	-0.00030	0.06
Monthly income	-0.00118	0.01
Multifamily unit	-0.02018	0.46
Private insurance	-0.03497	1.67
FHA-235 loan	-0.06886	1.25

*Statistically significant at the 0.95 level.
**Employment variables shown separately in table 4.2.
Source: Regression analysis.

over 90 percent is 0.08235 and that of the L/V interval of 85 to 90 percent is 0.04421. Both coefficients are positive; and the over 90 percent coefficient of 0.08235 being larger than the 85 to 90 percent coefficient of 0.04421 indicates that default risk increases as the L/V ratio increases. The base interval is not shown in table 4.1, because its coefficient is assigned a value of zero. The size of the over 90 percent coefficient is almost twice the size of the 85 to 90 percent coefficient, which indicates that relative to the base interval, a loan with an L/V ratio of over 90 percent is almost twice as risky as a loan with an L/V ratio of 85 to 90 percent. The L/V ratio of over 90 percent is shown to be highly significant with an F ratio of 16.75. The results support the a priori belief that the higher the L/V ratio, the greater the risk of default, and that loans with very high L/V ratios, for example, over 90 percent, are much more likely to default because of the very low initial equity at risk.

While previous studies have drawn attention to the fact that loan risk tends to increase with the loan-to-value ratio, confirming a widely held belief by practitioners and economists alike, the high sensitivity of this risk to high loan-to-value ratios is conspicuous. FHA, VA, and private mortgage insurance intuitively recognize this sensitivity to varying degrees.

The ratio of the borrower's monthly mortgage service payments to the borrower's monthly income is shown to be another very important variable. The two intervals shown in table 4.1 have positive coefficients, and the P/I interval of over 30 percent, having a coefficient of 0.09180, is very significant with an F ratio of 7.80 and is over three times that of the P/I interval of 22 to 30 percent, with a coefficient of 0.02703. This also indicates that default risk increases as the P/I ratio increases, and that loans with P/I ratios of over 30 percent are three times as likely to be in default when compared with loans with P/I ratios between 22 and 30 percent. This demonstrates that default risk increases more than proportionately with large P/I ratios.

The most important explanation for this result is that high fixed claims on income reduce an individual's ability to absorb financial adversity, a phenomenon that is measured in business finance by the ratio called "times fixed charges earned," where, all other things being given, low values are associated with high risks of insolvency.

It is usually felt that the age of the mortgagor may have an effect on default risk. The age factor is divided into three intervals believed to represent different stages of maturity and family responsibility. The results give mixed evidence of the age effect. Relative to the 30 to 50 age group used as the base for comparison, the over 50 age group is significantly riskier, while the under 30 age group is less risky, but not significantly so, at the 95 percent level. One possible explanation for the riskiness of the over 50 age group is the nonhomogeneous nature of the group. While the 50 to 60 age group may be very stable financially, the over 60 age group may not be very stable because of early retirement and retirement at 65 years and the financial instability that may result from the financial burden of catastrophic illness as age advances, which can easily constrain the ability of elderly mortgagors to meet their financial obligations. Retirees usually live in older neighborhoods where housing values may be declining. When housing values decline below the mortgage balance, a less costly alternative is for the mortgagor to default, or simply walk away from the mortgage. This is a phenomenon more often associated with inner city neighborhoods.

The number of years a borrower has been with the current employer before obtaining a mortgage is associated with income stability from stable employment. The practice of acquiring seniority, length of service, and vesting of pension rights all point toward longevity in employment as desirable and warranted. Since employment stability is an indicator of income stability, default risk should decline as the number of years with the current employer increases. The negative coefficient confirms this, and the F ratio of 15.76 makes it highly significant.

Older structures on mortgaged properties are usually located in older neighborhoods with declining property values. In cases where the property value has declined to less than the outstanding mortgage balance, the mortgagor might find it less costly to default by walking away from the mortgage obligation than to incur additional cost in selling the property and then having to make up for the shortfall in the price. The result shows that the age of the property tends to increase risk somewhat but is not a significant factor, as indicated by the very low value of the F ratio.

The presence of junior financing at the time the mortgage is executed increases the total amount of claims on the mortgaged property and the chances for the mortgagor to default, since a default in any one of the obligations could precipitate a foreclosure against the property. The regression coefficient is pretty sizable at 0.19653 and is very significant with an F ratio of 13.75. Junior financing, apparently, exerts a notable influence on the incidence of default, where it has the effect of increasing, or adjusting, an understated loan-to-loan-value ratio.

The unemployment rate has the largest positive and statistically significant coefficient, which makes it one of the most important explanatory factors, if not the single most important factor, in default risk. As the rate of unemployment in a community rises from people being laid off, mortgage default will be expected to rise as unemployed mortgagors find it increasingly difficult to service their outstanding mortgages. Properties put up for sale when there is high unemployment in the community may not fetch attractive prices sufficient to pay off their mortgages. When there is national or regional economic recession and depression, unemployment rises and consumers cut back on their purchases, thereby causing prices to fall. In this environment, unemployed mortgagors having difficulty servicing their mortgages would find it difficult to sell their homes or to get good prices to pay off their mortgages when they did sell them, in which case they might decide to default. Accordingly, as the unemployment rate rises, the rate of default rises rapidly as the incidence of default mounts.

It would normally be expected that increases in per capita changes in crimes against property would increase the risk of default as residents abandon their homes and move out of those areas with high crime rates. But the evidence from the regression analysis turns out to the contrary. This explanatory factor carries a negative sign and is not significant in default risk. A rational explanation for its negative correlation with default risk is that crimes against property are much higher in wealthier and more stable neighborhoods within the city limits and in the suburban communities, where default rates are lower.

VA insurance would appear to have virtually no influence whatsoever on default risk. This seems reasonable since veterans do not like to blemish their records with a default because they would like to continue to enjoy the many services and programs of the VA.

The presence of FHA insurance in a loan is shown to reduce the risk of default from the negative sign of the coefficient. The FHA provides a process that compensates lenders for loans that go bad; these loans are cleared in the lenders' records and may appear in good status. Since the realization of default risk is the actual dollar loss, because the lender obtains restitution from the FHA, it would appear that there is no risk. The presence of FHA insurance assures the lender that, whatever happens, FHA will make sure that the lender is repaid. It, therefore, can be seen to reduce the risk of default. This explanatory factor is highly significant.

An FHA-235 loan has a negative sign to indicate its decreasing effect on default risk, but is not a significant factor.

The price of the property is another variable that has a statistically significant risk-decreasing influence on the mortgaged property, indicating that default risk decreases as the price of property rises. This negative relationship of price to default risk is rational, since purchasers of higher-priced homes have higher incomes and these homes are located in relatively stable and newer neighborhoods within the city and suburbs. In addition, the price embodies the proper mix of the attributes in all of the explanatory factors discussed. Purchasers of high-priced property are screened with greater care and tend to have high net worths and incomes.

The number of children in the mortgagor's household increases the risk of default, but is shown not to be a significant factor. The financial resources of large families are burdened, but they manage to hold on to their properties to keep the roof over their heads.

Refinanced loans are frequently taken out by borrowers who may be in financial difficulties. The presence of a refinanced loan is shown in the regression analysis to increase the risk of default, and it is a very significant factor. Refinancing is frequently used for bill consolidation, after which the borrowers usually go on and run up more bills that, in effect, return the borrowers to the previous state of financial distress, which precipitates default.

The longer the term of the loan, the lower is the risk of default. This is the result obtained from the regression analysis, but the term factor is shown to have virtually no significance in the determination of default risk.

Higher monthly income decreases the risk of default because the mortgagor has more financial resources to work with. The evidence from the regression analysis supports this view, but shows that monthly income has no significant effect on default risk. This may be due in part to the fact that the nonlinear effects of the payment-to-income ratio have more significance than the monthly income itself in default risk.

Mortgaged properties are classified into single-family and two- or four-family units, with those containing five or more household units excluded from the analysis. The excluded units are considered more of a commercial business and do not fit into the ordinary household investment category. With the single-family property chosen as a base for comparison of relative riskiness, the result shows that default risk is reduced when loans are made for multifamily financing, and the effect is significant. It would appear that the income potential of the multifamily units provides for financial stability.

Private insurance in a loan is shown to reduce the risk of default, but it did not exhibit any significant effect on default risk. This may be due to the fact that borrowers are prescreened very carefully before private insurance is issued, to minimize the insurer's exposure.

The type of occupation or profession that one is engaged in is a proxy for income stability and income. Some occupations are perceived to be riskier than others, and lenders have experienced foreclosure problems with greater frequency in particular occupational groups. To detect this relative riskiness among various occupations, 18 occupations were identified as covering general occupational types. The 18 occupations are classified into six categories based on

Table 4.2
Coefficients and *F* Ratios of Occupation Qualitative Factors:* Default Risk

Occupation Group	Coefficient	F Ratio
1. Executive and middle management	−0.00291	0.02
2. Teacher or professor	0.00639	0.03
3. Government, military, and pensioned	0.02891	0.82
4. Insurance salesmen, other salesmen, arts, and clerical	0.01421	0.45
5. Own business, farmer, manufacturer's representative, speculative builder, and unskilled labor	0.05837**	8.83

*The sixth occupation group: professional, skilled labor, and building tradesman, not shown in the table, is used as the base group for qualitative comparison with the other five groups shown in the table.

**Denotes significance at the 95% level.

common attributes between occupational types, and a factor was assigned to each of the six occupational classes, as indicated in table 4.2. Since there is no formal basis for classifying the occupational types, other classifications could do just as well. The sixth class consisting of professionals, skilled labor, and building tradesmen is the base class against which the other occupational groups are compared. From the regression results presented in table 4.2, only the fifth class consisting of business proprietor, farmer, manufacturer's representative, speculative builder, and unskilled labor has a significant coefficient. The positive coefficient indicates that this occupational group is significantly riskier than the base group. Although occupational classes 2 to 4 are shown to be riskier than the base class from their positive coefficients, they are not of any significance. The first occupational class consisting of executives and middle management, on the other hand, is shown to be less risky, though not to any significant degree. It is possible that the class groups as constructed may have affected the relative risk effects observed and their degree of significance.

Summary of Significant Factors in Default Risk

Table 4.3 summarizes the factors shown to be significant at the 95 percent level, with their signs. Factors that enhance default risk are a loan-to-value ratio

Table 4.3
Variables Shown to Be Important in Foreclosure Analysis

Variables	Sign of Coefficient
Loan-to-loan-value ratio over 90%	+
Payment-to-income ratio over 30%	+
Age of mortgagor over 50	+
Presence of junior financing	+
Neighborhood unemployment rate	+
Presence of FHA insurance	−
Price of property	−
Refinanced loan	+
Presence of occupational group 5	+
Length of employment with current employer	−

of over 90 percent, a payment-to-income ratio of over 30 percent, the over 50 age group, the presence of junior financing, the neighborhood unemployment rate, the presence of a refinanced loan, and the presence of occupational group 5. Factors reducing default are lengthy employment with current employer prior to date of mortgage, the presence of FHA insurance, and higher-priced properties.

Another perspective is afforded by suggesting a profile, in a loose sense, of a person likely to default. Such a person will tend to have a very high loan-to-value ratio and a high payment-to-income ratio, will live in a neighborhood with a high unemployment rate, will have either junior financing or a refinanced loan, will have a low-priced property, will have been employed with the current employer for a relatively short period, will not have FHA insurance, and will be in both occupation group 5 and the over 50 age group at the time the loan is made.

EMPIRICAL RESULTS: DELINQUENCY RISK

The regression results for delinquency risk are presented in table 4.4. The table shows the factors, the values of the coefficients obtained from the regression analysis, and their F ratios. The R^2 and the overall F ratio for this regression are 0.386 and 7.386, respectively.[9]

The L/V ratio is a very important explanatory factor in delinquency risk. As shown in table 4.4, a loan with an L/V ratio over 90 percent is significantly risky relative to a loan with an L/V ratio less than 85 percent in the base group used for comparison. This result supports the evidence that high L/V ratios normally require high monthly-payment-to-monthly-income ratios, and given the mortgagor's family financial responsibilities, it may become difficult to meet the monthly mortgage service and other financial obligations punctually. In contrast, the much lower L/V ratio of the under 85 percent base group should have relatively lower monthly-payment-to-monthly-income ratios and correspondingly lower delinquency rates. Loans with an 85 to 90 percent L/V ratio are also riskier than the base group, but less riskier than loans with over a 90 percent L/V ratio, as would be expected, but not significantly so.

The monthly-payment-to-monthly-income ratio is another very important factor in delinquency risk, and the relationship is very direct. The mortgagor has to make the monthly mortgage service payments. A high monthly payment relative to the mortgagor's monthly income leaves a smaller proportion of the income available to meet the family's other financial obligations and financial emergencies. Mortgage payment may be delayed when financial emergencies arise, resulting in delinquency. This line of reasoning is borne out by the results in table 4.4, showing that P/I ratios over 30 percent are significantly riskier than P/I ratios less than 22 percent, the base group. Loans with P/I ratios between 22 and 30 percent are shown to have more risk from the positive coefficient relative to the base group with P/I ratios less than 22 percent, but the risk is not significant.

The age of the mortgagor is treated first as a level term for the whole factor, and then the factor is divided up into three age groups to see if there are any differences between the age groups in rates of delinquency. The results show that

Table 4.4
Coefficients and _F_ Ratios of Explanatory Variables in Delinquency Risk

Factor	Coefficient	F Ratio
Loan to Loan Value:		
Over 90%	0.48730*	9.13468
85 - 90%	0.21532	1.67422
Payment to Income:		
Over 30%	0.96224*	16.06260
22 - 30%	0.24256	0.56792
Age of Mortgagor:	−0.01079*	7.70573
Over 50	0.21381*	4.25448
Less than 30	−0.06516	1.10215
Number of Years with Employer	0.00183	0.33521
Age of Property	0.00317*	5.47683
Unemployment Rate	−0.66183	0.48623
Per Capita Changes in Crimes Against Property	−0.95608	0.14831
Per Capita Changes in Crimes Against Persons	19.20426	0.55920
VA Insurance	0.61604*	75.99899
FHA Insurance	0.07133	1.33797
Price of Property**	−0.00081	1.48555
Number of Children	0.4610 *	12.48346
Refinanced Loan	0.28278*	8.78546
Term of Loan	−0.00457	0.61744
Monthly Income**	−0.04422	0.01106
Private Insurance	−0.00002	1.0531
% Change in Population	−0.18848	4.14393

*Statistically significant at the 0.95 level.

**Expressed in dollar amounts. To express in thousands of dollars, move decimal point three places to the right. Dollar values deflated by the consumer price index.

delinquency is inversely related to age; that is, as age increases, delinquency rates decline to a significant degree. When compared with the 30 to 50 age group, the over 50 age group appears riskier, and to a significant degree. This may be due to the nonhomogeneity of the over 50 age group, with the over 60 age subgroup having higher rates of delinquency.

Another explanation is that higher-income groups found within the over 50 age group include a high proportion of the executive occupational class who are sometimes slow in making monthly service payments for a variety of reasons. The under 30 age group has a lower rate of delinquency than the 30 to 50 age group, as shown by the negative sign of the coefficient, but this lower rate was not significant. The negative relationship between age and rates of delinquency shown in the coefficient of the level term reflects to a significant degree the low rates of delinquency of the 30 to 50 age group used as the base for comparison.

Ordinarily, one would suspect that the longer the years of service with an employer (the more stable the employment), the lower the rate of delinquency. The evidence from the regression results shows that delinquency rates increase with years of service incorporated in the factor of number of years with employer, although the result is not statistically significant.

The age of property factor is shown to be positively correlated with delinquency in a very significant way. One possible reason is that older properties are usually located in inner city neighborhoods occupied by low-income people with high L/V ratios over 90 percent and P/I ratios over 30 percent. The over 50 age groups normally occupy older homes where they have lived for many years. This age group is shown to have higher rates of delinquency than younger age groups.

While higher unemployment rates are directly correlated with higher rates of default, they are shown to be negatively correlated with delinquency, although this relationship is not significant. It would appear that mortgagors make all efforts to protect their investment in their homes, particularly during times of unemployment, by keeping up with their monthly service payments on a punctual basis. Another explanation is that lenders located in areas susceptible to periodic unemployment may work out plans with the unemployed during periods of rising unemployment that require payment of interest only during the receipt of unemployment compensation and permit postponement of mortgage payments when the compensation runs out. The mortgage interest is added to the principal balance, and repayment resumes when the mortgagor returns to work. While helping the unemployed, the suspension of payments is also in the lender's interest, since the alternative is possible foreclosure.

Another factor of interest that is negatively correlated with delinquency rates is per capita changes in crimes against property. This factor, as seen previously, is a surrogate for higher-income groups situated in fashionable neighborhoods within the city and suburbs with valuable household articles for robbers to steal. These groups in general have lower rates of delinquency, reflected by the size of the coefficient.

Per capita changes in crimes against persons, on the other hand, is a surrogate for lower-income groups located in areas of much crime associated with personal assault and bodily injuries. This factor shows a very high positive correlation with delinquency, as would be expected, although the relationship is not statistically significant.

VA insurance has a strong positive correlation with delinquency, as shown by the positive coefficient and the very high F ratio of 75.99 in table 4.4. Mortgages to veterans generally carry very high L/V ratios in the over 90 percent range, resulting in high payment-to-income ratios in the over 30 percent range, which make the group relatively very risky; hence, the need for the VA special insurance. A sizable proportion of veterans usually have rather lengthy periods of adjustment following service, during which financial emergencies frequently occur, leading to delinquency.

The FHA insurance factor also has a positive correlation with delinquency, as expected, owing to some of the same reasons as cited for VA insurance, but the relationship is shown not to be statistically significant.

The factor of price of property has a negative sign to indicate that as price increases, the rate of delinquency decreases; but this relationship is not a significant one. Higher-priced properties are bought by higher-income mortgagors with adequate financial resources to meet financial emergencies. This group maintains high credit worthiness by paying up their bills punctually.

Large families usually have large financial obligations since it costs more to maintain larger families with growing children. With constant pressure on the family's resources, financial emergencies usually require reallocating resources and delaying payment on some periodic obligations, such as mortgage service. Such delays result in delinquencies and slow payments. The regression results show a positive coefficient that is statistically significant for number of children.

Another factor that is positively correlated with delinquency and is statistically significant is refinanced loan. This is to be expected since refinancing is done on loans that have been in financial difficulty or for bill consolidation purposes. It is frequently the case that after bill consolidation refinancing, the borrower usually ends up with more bills and greater obligations than before the refinancing.[10]

As the term of loan increases, the mortgage is presumed to mature and the chances for delinquency diminish. The evidence from the regression bears this relationship out from the negative coefficient, which turns out not to be statistically significant.

Similarly, as monthly income increases, the borrower's capacity to meet financial obligations increases, the monthly-payment-to-monthly-income ratio decreases, and rates of delinquency fall.

Percentage change in population is a location factor reflecting population dynamics. In areas where there is rising population, the percentage change in population is positive. These are usually growth areas witnessing housing and neighborhood growth and development and economic vibrancy, which in turn foster high employment rates and rising incomes. The factor of percentage change in population is therefore a locational surrogate for new or growing neighborhoods within the city limits, in the suburbs, and in the contiguous rural counties. The evidence from the regression shows that such environments usually have a significant declining effect on rates of delinquency.

The coefficients and F ratios of the occupation factors in the regression analysis for delinquency risks are presented in table 4.5. There are 18 occupations, 15 of which are presented there, with executives not shown, used as the base for the comparison. Two occupational types—farm labor and special builder—were not represented in the loan sample used in the regression analysis.

Fourteen of the 15 occupations reported in table 4.5 have coefficients with negative signs to indicate that in comparison with executives, the base, each of

Table 4.5
Coefficients and F Ratios of Occupation Factors in Delinquency Risk

Occupation	Coefficient	F Ratio
Middle Management	−0.20314*	3.99610
Professional	−0.13554	1.92013
Own Business	−0.13568	0.95651
Building Trades	−0.18345	1.11595
Insurance Salesman	−0.14401	0.62620
Other Salesman	−0.13575	1.49845
Clerical	−0.24654*	3.70128
Teacher	−0.12772	0.72687
Arts	0.33109*	3.72832
Skilled Labor	−0.13968	1.70890
Unskilled Labor	−0.13968	1.70890
Military	−0.16965	0.16433
Government	−0.29389*	5.19538
Manufacturer's Representative	−0.11836	0.33265
Pensioned	−0.03256	0.01736

*Denotes significance at the 95% level.

Note: The executive occupational type is the base occupation against which other occupations are to be compared.

the occupations exhibited lower rates of delinquency and therefore have lower
delinquency risk. However, only three coefficients are statistically significant.
At first glance, this result might seem erroneous because executives are associated with high incomes, stable employment, superior financial responsibility,
and credit worthiness. It is evident that for a variety of reasons some executives
are somewhat tardy in the way they make their monthly mortgage service payments. Executives travel frequently and may miss their scheduled payment dates.
In general, executives can readily afford the late payment penalty fee, which
serves as an incentive to other occupational types with lower income to pay the
monthly installments on time. Some see the monthly payments as bothersome
and pay quarterly or some other monthly combinations in arrears.

The three occupational types with negative coefficients that are statistically
significant are middle management, clerical, and government employees. Middle management comprises the organizational men, with a growing family living
in high-income areas of the city and in suburbia. This group is upwardly bound,
interested in protecting their credit worthiness as well as family and social status.
Since they pay their bills punctually, they exhibit lower rates of delinquency.
Clerical employees represent stable employment. A high proportion of clerical
employees are women who take meticulous care to maintain their credit worthiness by paying up their bills punctually. Government employees include a cross
spectrum of executive, middle management, professional, and clerical groups
with stable employment and relatively good income. The cross section of government employees has a reputation of paying their bills on time, which significantly lowers delinquency rates. Late payment penalties are a significant induce-
ment to avoid delinquency by these three groups.

One occupational type—arts—is shown to have a positive coefficient that is
statistically significant, indicating that it is riskier than executives, the base
group. A significant proportion of those engaged in professional arts are free-
lance self-employed types who do not have stable employment and a consistent
source of income. Punctual payments of monthly mortgage service installments
are interrupted during periods of unstable employment.

Summary of Significant Factors in Delinquency Risk

Table 4.6 summarizes the factors shown to be significant at the 95 percent
level with their signs. Factors that enhance delinquency risk are a loan-to-value
ratio of over 90 percent, a payment-to-income ratio of over 30 percent, the over
50 age group, the presence of VA insurance, the family size in number of
children, and the presence of a refinanced loan. Factors reducing delinquency are
the under 50 age group, the age of the property, neighborhoods with higher
percentage rate of change in population, and mortgagors in one of the following
four occupations: middle management, clerical, arts, and government service.

Another perspective can be gained from a suggested profile, in a loose sense,
of a person likely to be delinquent. Such a person will tend to have a very high
loan-to-value ratio and a high payment-to-income ratio, will be in the over 50 age

Table 4.6
Factors Important in Delinquency Analysis

Factors	Sign of Coefficient
Loan to Loan Value over 90%	+
Payment to Income over 30%	+
Age of Mortgagor	−
Age of Mortgagor over 50	+
Age of Property	−
VA Insurance	+
Number of Children	+
Refinanced Loan	+
% Change in Population	−
Middle Management	−
Clerical	−
Arts	+
Government	−

Source: From tables 4.4 and 4.5.

group, will have VA insurance, will have a large family, will have a refinanced loan, is not living in a recently vintage home, is not living in a neighborhood experiencing rapid increases in population, and is not employed in middle management, clerical, the arts, or government service at the time the loan is made.

SIGNIFICANT FACTORS COMMON TO DEFAULT AND DELINQUENCY RISKS

There are four factors that are significant in both default and delinquency risks. They are a very high loan-to-value ratio, a high payment-to-income ratio, the over 50 age group, and a refinanced loan.

NOTES

1. J. P. Herzog and J. S. Earley, *Home Mortgages Delinquency and Foreclosure* (New York: National Bureau of Economic Research, 1970), is a previous study that used the linear probability model. This is an aggregative study dealing with the national mortgage market.

2. R. G. McGillivray, "Estimating the Linear Probability Function," *Econometrica* 38 (1970): pp. 775–77.

3. S. M. Goldfeld and R. E. Quandt, *Nonlinear Methods in Econometrics* (Amsterdam: North Holland, 1973); James L. Kenkel, "A Monte Carlo Study of Some Small Sample Properties of Estimators of the Linear Probability Function," Econometric Society ASSA Meetings (delivered December 29, 1973); V. K. Smith and C. J. Cicchetti, "Regression Analysis with Dichotomous Dependent Variables," Econometric Society ASSA Meetings (delivered December 29, 1973).

4. When the actual dollar loss is available for each loan, it is preferable to use this as the dependent factor, rather than the actual foreclosure. The use of foreclosure produces an index of foreclosure.

5. Information about the present status of the loan only is usually available. For example, a loan that was once delinquent, but presently is paid up, is classified as a good loan rather than as a delinquent loan. The past payment history would be available to determine if a loan was ever delinquent in the past, even if it was presently paid up. Some of the loans classified as good loans may have been delinquent some time in the past.

6. Other types of transformations can be used, of course, to detect nonlinear effects. Squaring and the taking of logarithms to measure nonlinearities were attempted, but the use of dummy variables produced the best results. Stepwise regression is not used because the significance of any variable may change drastically by the inclusion of any other explanatory variable.

7. The results presented here represent a part of a study conducted under the auspices and specifications set forth by the Federal Savings and Loan Insurance Corporation. However, the results stated herein do not necessarily represent those of the FSLIC. Alex O. Williams, William Beranek, Robert F. Byrne, James Kenkel, and David Pentico, *A Study of the Factors Associated with, or Contributing to, Risk in Urban Mortgage Lending* (Pittsburgh: University of Pittsburgh, 1973).

8. The loan value of R^2 is the result of the relatively low number of foreclosures in the sample, which did not allow for much explanatory power. Because of the carrying cost and banking examination reports, lending institutions only foreclose in extraneous cases.

9. The R^2 value of .386 indicates that approximately 39 percent of variation of delinquency is explained by the explanatory factors used. In light of the pre-selection process used by lenders this is considered very satisfactory explanatory power.

10. Refinancing may decrease delinquency risk when it is done to lower high mortgage interest rates.

CHAPTER 5

Cohort Analysis of Delinquency Risk

Cohort analysis divides mortgage loans into risk classes and provides a useful method for quantifying risk factors and determining the reliability of these factors for the prediction of delinquency risk. The cohort method assigns each mortgage loan to cohorts, or groups, in the year of origination. Each cohort is defined by a combination of attributes from a range of values of specified variables. For example, in any year of origination, say 19X0, mortgages are grouped by each of a specified range of loan-to-value ratios and income (Y) classes. Two other characteristics used in the grouping process are (1) the age of the collateral asset of the mortgage—(a) new or (b) existing—and (2) the location of the asset—(a) inside or (b) outside the urban metropolitan area. A major cohort is therefore defined for each combination of the values of the loan-to-value ratio and income, as well as the age and location of the asset. The number of mortgages in a cohort is the sum of all mortgages issued in a given year that possess the same characteristic combination of the four factors.

DELINQUENT MORTGAGES

A mortgage is classified as delinquent if it is 40 days past the due date of payment or 70 days since the last payment. For example, if payment was due on October 1, but has not been received by December 10, the mortgage is classified as delinquent on December 10 and transferred to the delinquent status group for appropriate action. A notation is made in each mortgage file of the first delinquency only.

The Rate of Delinquency

The rate of delinquency for a cohort is calculated by dividing the number of delinquencies by the years of occurrence for each cohort by the number of original mortgages in that cohort. For example, assume that the number of delinquencies in cohort Q in year 19X2 is 15, and the number of original mortgages in cohort Q in the year of origination, 19X0, is 1,000. Then the rate of delinquency in year 19X2 for cohort Q is 15/1,000 = 0.015. To express this proportion as a percentage, it is multiplied by 100. Thus,

$$\text{rate of delinquency in cohort Q in 19X2} = \frac{\text{delinquencies in cohort Q in 19X2}}{\text{total mortgages in cohort Q}} \times 100$$

$$= \frac{15}{1,000} \times 100$$

$$= 1.5 \text{ percent.}$$

In a case where there are no delinquencies in a cohort in a given year, the rate of delinquency would be 0 percent. However, a negligible positive value such as 0.1 percent would be assigned in this case to permit a transformation of this value to logarithms to be used in the regression analysis.

Delinquency Risk and Economic and Financial Effects

The delinquency experience of a lending institution with particular mortgage cohorts would definitely influence its current lending behavior. It would therefore be of interest to examine the effects of some economic and financial characteristics on delinquency risk to gain some insights into the key factors that could be utilized to predict delinquency risk.

THE REGRESSION RELATIONSHIP

There are two types of factors that influence the delinquency risk of mortgages. They can be generally classified as those that can be measured quantitatively and those that are qualitative.

Quantitative Factors

Continuous Independent Variables

Loan-to-Value Ratio

The original loan-to-value ratio at the inception of a mortgage indicates the amount of the loan relative to the value of the property. The difference between the value of the house and the loan is the amount of equity available to protect the mortgage in its initial years from the effects of a significant decline in real estate prices.

Example 5.1.   A borrower wants to purchase a house valued at $100,000 with a down payment of $5,000 and a loan of $95,000.

$$\text{initial L/V ratio} = \frac{\text{loan}}{\text{value}} = \frac{95,000}{100,000} = 95 \text{ percent.}$$

Suppose the house value declined by 5 percent in year 2, and the loan has been paid down by $1,000.

$$\text{L/V ratio} = \frac{94,000}{95,000} = 98.95 \text{ or } 99 \text{ percent.}$$

For any given level of loan in a mortgage, as the price of house drops, the L/V ratio will rise. A precipitous drop in prices will cause the L/V ratio to rise, as in example 5.1. A decline in the value of the property for any reason means that it would take a larger proportion of the sale proceeds to repay the outstanding loan than before the decline in value. A precipitous drop in the value would require a significantly higher percentage of the sale proceeds to pay off the loan. If the decline in the value of the house as reflected in the current market price approaches the loan amount, the incentive for the mortgagor to default increases. And this would depend upon whether or not the closing costs of the sale would be covered by the sale proceeds or would be out of pocket. If the sale proceeds are not enough to cover closing costs, then the mortgagor may find it less expensive to walk away from the mortgage contract and default.

A large down payment means a higher equity interest in the property by the mortgagor and a lower initial L/V ratio. The higher the equity interest, or equity shield, the longer it will take for a price decline to depress the value of the property to the point where it would be to the mortgagor's advantage to default.

Example 5.2. A large down payment reduces the initial L/V ratio while increasing the initial equity-to-value ratio. The higher equity interest shields the lender from default risk exposure, as shown in the following two cases. Assume the purchase price of the property was $100,000.

In *case 5.1,*

Loan = $90,000 $\text{L/V} = \frac{90,000}{100,000} = 90 \text{ percent}$

Down payment = equity = $10,000 $\text{E/V} = \frac{10,000}{100,000} = 10 \text{ percent}$

Closing costs = 2 percent   Sales fee = 6 percent

The E/V ratio is the shield to protect the mortgagee, because the market price of the house could fall up to 10 percent before the equity is wiped out and the loan to realizable value of 100 percent. Taking into consideration closing costs of 2 percent and a selling fee of 6 percent, the equity shield is only 2 percent. If the market price drops 2 percent, with 2 percent closing costs and a selling fee of 6 percent, the mortgagor would end up with nothing from the sale of the house. Should the market price drop another 1 percent, the mortgagor would have to pay another 1 percent out of pocket to meet the 2 percent closing costs. The mortgagor may not wish to incur the additional 1 percent out-of-pocket cost, and might choose to minimize his losses by walking away from the mortgage by defaulting.

In *case 5.2,*

Loan = \$80,000	$L/V = \dfrac{80,000}{100,000} = 80$ percent
Equity = \$20,000	$E/V = \dfrac{20,000}{100,000} = 20$ percent
Closing costs = 2 percent	Selling fee = 6 percent.

The higher equity of \$20,000 provides a 20 percent equity shield. With closing costs of 2 percent and a selling fee of 6 percent, the market price could drop up to 12 percent without the mortgagor having to incur any out-of-pocket costs on the sale of the house. If the price drops by 13 percent, the mortgagor might have an incentive to vacate the mortgage by default.

Borrowers with limited financial resources prefer to make lower down payment, resulting in a higher L/V ratio. But a borrower with limited resources will have difficulty coping when serious temporary financial problems arise, which may lead to delinquencies. The borrower will make up the delinquencies as the financial problems are alleviated. It is likely that delinquency may recur several times during the life of the mortgage, if the financial resources of the mortgagor do not improve. However, as the equity grows through the appreciation of the property, the incentive to keep the mortgage current will increase. There is not a direct relationship between delinquency and the L/V ratio, as in the case of default, but there is an indirect relationship that makes the L/V ratio, through its reciprocal, the E/V ratio, an important factor in determining the likelihood of delinquency.

The expected effect of the seasoning of the mortgage on delinquency rates is not as obvious as in the case of default, since not all delinquencies culminate in default. As the mortgage ages, the greater is the probability that it will not become delinquent in subsequent years.

Age of Mortgage

The age of the mortgage is expected to influence delinquency rates. The longer a family has resided at a given address and the longer it has met its payments on schedule, the greater the probability that its mortgage will not become delinquent in subsequent years. First, as the mortgage has matured, the family's liquid assets will have been rebuilt following the investment in the house at the time of purchase. Second, the family has displayed over the years financial responsibility that identifies it as a superior credit risk that it would like to maintain; it has also developed neighborhood relationships as well as a pattern of stability over the years that it might not want to interrupt. Because of these factors, seasoning of the mortgage should lower the expected annual incidence of first delinquencies.

Monthly Income of Mortgagor

The income of the mortgagor is an important factor because it is an indication of two things: (1) the income available to the mortgagor to meet the mortgage payments and all other family expenses and (2) its relationship to the total assets of the mortgagor. Generally, the higher the income, the greater the total assets available to weather financial adversity. The financial assets of low-income families are at disproportionately lower levels compared with high-income families.[1]

Value Transformation and Class Medians

Table 5.1 presents the original loan-to-value ratio and the annual mortgagor income classes, as well as the transformed values of the class medians adopted. The original data is divided into 10 classes with some classes having too few observations to use in the analysis. The 10 classes were collapsed into the 5 classes shown in the table for the L/V ratio and the income classes. The expected shapes of the frequency profiles of both the L/V ratio and the income are taken into consideration in assigning the class medians. The frequencies of the L/V ratio decline from the highest class, over 80 percent, to the lowest class, 60 percent or less, with a median L/V ratio of 79 percent in the sample of loans. The sample median of mortgagor's income is $9,900. A greater proportion of the incomes fell between $9,601 and $14,400, which made up the third and fourth classes.

The median of the over 80 percent class was obtained by dividing the number of loans with L/V ratios over 80 percent by 2, and the L/V ratio of the middle loan was 0.88. Subtracting the L/V ratio from 1.0 gives the E/V ratio, the amount of equity paid by the mortgagor when the mortgage was taken out. Subtracting 0.88 from 1.0 gives 0.12, which is then multiplied by 10 to convert

Table 5.1
Original Loan-to-Value Ratio and Annual Mortgagor Income Classes and Transformed Values of the Class Medians Adopted

Loan-to-Value Ratio L/V	10(1 − L/V) = (E/V)10	Mortgagor Income (Y)	Y/1000
Over 80%	1.2	$7,200 and less	6.0
76% − 80%	2.2	7,201 − 9,600	8.5
69% − 75%	2.8	9,601 − 12,000	10.8
61% − 68%	3.5	12,001 − 14,400	13.0
60% and less	4.5	Over 14,400	18.0

Residential Mortgages

Table 5.2
Distribution of Mortgages in the Sample: Inside and Outside Central County by New and Existing Properties

Year of Origination	Inside Central County			Outside Central County		
	New	Existing	Total	New	Existing	Total
19X0	11	43	54	7	2	9
19X1	231	656	887	53	99	152
19X2	76	504	580	10	82	92
19X3	36	743	779	7	105	112
19X4	110	774	884	25	106	131
19X5	67	426	493	7	59	66
19X6	134	434	568	22	30	52
19X7	26	468	494	6	37	43
19X8	173	313	486	26	33	59
19X9	64	688	752	20	88	108
19Y1	84	562	646	30	73	103
19Y2	14	38	52	2	5	7
Total:	1,026	5,649	6,675	215	719	934
Percentage N/E:	15.37	84.63	100	23.02	76.98	100
Percentage I=0*:	13.48	74.24	87.72	2.83	9.45	12.28

*The total number of mortgages in the sample is 7,609.

N=New, E=Existing, I=Inside, O=Outside

the fraction into a whole number of 1.2. The other L/V ratio medians were computed in the same way.

The median income of the $7,200 and less class was obtained by dividing the number of loans with income of $7,200 or less by 2; the median income obtained was $6,000. Dividing the median income of $6,000 by $1,000 to get 6 reduces the large income figures to smaller numbers of comparable size to the L/V medians.

Table 5.2 presents the distribution of mortgages in the sample inside and outside the central county for new and existing loans. Of the 6,675 houses located inside the central county, new houses make up 15.37 percent, while existing houses make up 84.63 percent. In contrast, of the 934 mortgages outside the central county, new houses are 23.02 percent and existing houses 76.98 percent of the total. By comparison, mortgages for new houses make up a higher proportion of mortgages outside the central county than within. On the other hand, mortgages on new and existing homes located outside the central county make up only 12.28 percent of the total number of mortgages for houses both in and out of the central county for the 12-year period.

Qualitative Factors

Discontinuous Independent Variables

Qualitative factors involve all nonquantitative characteristics of the borrower, the property, and the lender that may help in identifying the type of risk being investigated, in this case delinquency risk. There are usually many qualitative factors that, in one way or another, can contribute to the identification of risk, with some contributing more than others depending upon the situation, type of risk, and amount of information or data available.

In this analysis, two qualitative factors of the exponential form e_x^a prior to logarithmic transformation have been identified as being useful in determining delinquency risk. They are (1) the location factor, which identifies whether the property to be mortgaged is situated within or outside the limits of the central county; and (2) the market status, which identifies the property as new or resale. This market status factor is also used to identify the age of the property: new and existing.

The function of the qualitative factor, which is called a "dummy variable" in statistical analysis, is to differentiate the intercept for subclasses. The location factor separates properties located in the central county ($x = 0$) from properties located outside the central county in the contiguous and outlying counties ($x = 1$). The age factor separates new properties ($c = 0$) from existing properties ($c = 1$) previously occupied by another family and in the market for resale.

The location factor is important for several reasons. Lenders holding construction financing made to speculative builders of new homes constructed prior to buyer's commitment may sometimes have to lower their credit standards to prospective buyers lined up by the builders in order to protect the construction financing. Lowering the credit standard likely results in higher rates of delinquency, and thus higher risk. In the case of FHA and VA loans in which a government agency gives the builder advance commitment to insure the loan, delinquency rates are more likely to occur.[2]

Existing homes may be presumed to be riskier than new homes, because as houses grow older they become less desirable owing to lack of the newer features of home design, equipment, and amenities, for example, the absence of air conditioning, the size of the plot, functional obsolescence, and the high cost of rehabilitating older homes relative to the housing values in their respective neighborhoods. Older homes require more frequent repairs that may overburden the financial resources of the mortgagor, and thus lead to delinquency.

Central cities' residential neighborhoods are prone to decay, while new suburban neighborhoods are developing and growing, which makes the central city location riskier. The location of the central city within the central county would make neighborhoods within the county somewhat less desirable and riskier than neighborhoods in contiguous counties. Since lenders in the inner city are conversant with the process of neighborhood deterioration, they may require compensating qualities of the property and of the borrower not recognized in the risk analysis presented here to make up for the detriment of some inner city locations before extending loans.

Since the qualitative location factors provide only for differences in level effects in relation to the size of the intercepts, they do not address the root causes of risk differences or help to identify differences in the structure of risk. Because of this limitation, risk difference resulting from the location of properties should not be interpreted very rigidly since the underlying causes have not been clearly identified and quantified. It would be difficult to make strict causal interpretations of the coefficients of location factors, because neither the central county nor the contiguous counties can be regarded as uniform from the point of view of home mortgage–lending risk. There are some very desirable neighborhoods and submarkets in cities, and some undesirable neighborhoods in the more mature suburban areas as well as in the rural towns of outlying counties. An analysis of the neighborhoods within the inner city is necessary to measure their diversity.

For this analysis, the delinquency rate is defined as 100 times the ratio of the number of delinquencies in any year and cohort to the number of mortgages originated in that cohort in year z. In our sample, z goes from 19X0 to 19Y2, where 19X0, 1, 2, . . . , 19X9, and 19Y0, 1, 2, . . . , 19Y9.[3]

For any year of origination, z, mortgages are grouped by each of a specified number of L/V ratio and income (Y) classes. Mortgages are also classified as "new" and "existing" (dummy variable c) and as "inside" or "outside" the central county (dummy variable x). A mortgage cohort is therefore defined for each combination of the values of L/V_i, y_j, c_k, x_m, and z_n. Counting all mortgages having one particular combination of these characteristics yields the number of mortgages in that cohort, $M_{i,j,k,m,n}$.

The annual delinquency rates are then calculated for a cohort by dividing delinquencies (D) in the year of origination and in all subsequent years by the original number of mortgages in that cohort. For example, assume that the number of mortgages originated in 19X0 ($z = 0$) and characterized by one specific combination of the values of L/V_i, y_j, c_k, and x_m is 100. Delinquencies in 19X0 will then occur at the average age of one-half year ($d = 0.5$). If there are no such delinquencies, the delinquency rate, $100(D_{0.5}/M)_{i,j,k,m,}Z_n = 0$, is set equal to a negligible positive value, such as 0.1, to allow log transformation. First delinquencies in 19X2 on the mortgages originated in 19X0 occur at an average age of one year ($d = 1$). If there are two such delinquencies on the 100 mortgages originally endorsed in that cohort, $100(D_1/M)$ (with the same subscripts attached) is equal to two.

Continuing the process for subsequent years, annual delinquency rates are constructed on mortgages originated in 19X0 from 19X0 through 19Y2, so that the total number of delinquency rates for $z = 0$ (19X0) is 12 across the various mortgage ages. For $z = 1$ (19X1) it is 11, and so on, until for $z = 11$ (19Y2), only delinquency rates in the same year can be registered. For each mortgage cohort defined by L/V$_i$, Y_j, c_k, and x_m, there is a maximum of 78 delinquency rates across the various years and ages.

Since mortgages are grouped into five loan-to-value ratio classes, five income classes, and two c and two x classes in the basic model, the maximum total number of delinquency rates is 7,800, if all cells can be filled. If $M < 12$ in any cohort, no reasonably continuous delinquency rate that contains the maximum number of mortgages that can possibly become delinquent would then be too small. The number of delinquency rates constructed from the complete data records on 7,609 mortgage originations is 1,236 under this criterion, rather than 7,800.[4]

From the relationship of delinquency age cohort observations to minimum numbers of mortgages in a cohort, the number of delinquency age cohort observations is 2,106 if the minimum number of mortgages in a cohort is required to be 6; 1,236 if it is 12; 780 if it is 20; and 432 if it is 30.[5] At that level of aggregation, the distinctions by c and x can no longer be made because of insufficient observations. Without these variables, the regression coefficients reported subsequently proved remarkably robust to variation in the choice of cutoff, so that 12 is used throughout. For example, if the cutoff is raised from 12 to 30, R^2 will rise (from 0.11 to 0.14), as is to be expected at higher levels of aggregation, but the size of the regression coefficients remains stable as their statistical significance grows.

The 1,236 annual delinquency rates that could be formed from the sample were based on an expected number of 1,236/6.5, or 190, mortgage cohorts, since first delinquencies were used to construct 6.5 annual delinquency rates, on the average. By contrast, the maximum number of cohorts obtained by the five-dimensional classification selected is 1,200 (the product of 5L/V, 5Y, 2c, 2x, and 12z classes), with a maximum of 300 cohorts for each of the four combinations of c and x.

The data in table 5.2 show that there are comparatively few new (N) house mortgages compared with existing (E) home mortgages and few outside (O) locations compared with locations inside (I) the central county. Only 18 cohorts containing 12 or more mortgages each could be constructed for the combination new and inside the central county (NI), 1 for new and outside the central county (NO), and 10 for existing and outside the central county (EO), compared with

149 [out of a maximum of 300 for existing homes inside the central county (EI)]. The actual number of cohorts in the sample, 178, is thus slightly less than 190, the number that would have been expected if the mortgage cohorts included in the regression had been distributed randomly with respect to the year of endorsement. The smaller number of actual cohorts obtained is a reasonable outcome since table 5.2 shows that originations in the sample were bunched in the older years, 19X1 and 19X4, in which a greater than average number of annual delinquencies could be observed to date. With some observations lost in cohorts with less than 12 mortgages, the actual average number of mortgages in each cohort is at most 7,609/178, or 43.

Problems of Small Sample Size

The arithmetic mean annual delinquency rate in the sample is 1.15 percent, and the probability of observing zero delinquencies on the 43 mortgages in a representative cohort is over 60 percent [since 0.000 approximates $0.0115 = 0.9883$ and $(0.9885)^{43} = 0.61$]. The large blocks of zeroes that occur across all risk classes lower the size and significance of the regression coefficients in comparison with estimates derived from much larger samples and in which delinquency rates do not remain bunched at measured values of zero. The discontinuities from the occurrence of zeroes inevitably lower the percentage of the total variation in delinquency rates (R^2) that can be explained by our estimates. Because of the small size of the sample, the number of risk classes or cohorts formed should be kept small. A larger sample would permit greater structural detail.

The small size of the sample limits the analysis in another respect. Recall that delinquency rates on cohorts containing less than 12 mortgages are not included in the regression, because most of the measured delinquency rates would have been zero. Measured delinquency rates can sometimes greatly exceed the mean if the denominator is small. Cohort analysis weights all delinquency rates equally, regardless of how many mortgages are contained in a cohort; therefore, the deviant observations on cohorts containing few mortgages count as much as the rates that can be calculated in a more continuous fashion on a larger body of data bases.

Correlation Among the Explanatory Variables

In the screening process, the required minimum number of mortgages per cohort is raised. While the number of variables and the ranges of the variables identified in the construction of the cohorts are unchanged, the number of data points falls, since more delinquency rates and mortgages are excluded from the regression. Fewer unusual combinations survive this screening. The advantage of cohort analysis, using the delinquency histories of individual mortgages as dependent variable, lies in its ability to erase whatever correlation might prevail between risk characteristics in the ungrouped data through the resulting cross-correlational statistical independence of the regression coefficients that enhance the process of calculating the risk index for cohorts within or beyond the observed range, and assures the stability of the regression coefficients.

For example, if low income of mortgagors is usually associated with high loan-to-value ratio financing,[6] then those low-income mortgagors who do not have high loan-to-value ratios may be considered exceptions. Cohort analysis will assign equal significance to these exceptions. In the cohort analysis, the loan-to-value ratio and income identification variables of cohorts would not be correlated, although the characteristics tend to be linked on individual mortgages. The loan-to-value ratio and income defining the remaining mortgage cohorts may again become correlated if many of the observations on the exceptional combinations are deleted.

The explanatory variables in the regression model, other than $ln(d)$ and d^2 (the correlation coefficient, R, is 0.79 in that case), are almost entirely uncorrelated, even after large numbers of cohorts are dropped because of insufficient observations. The logarithm of the equity-to-value ratio rises only very slightly with the logarithm of income ($R = 0.05$), and the correlation between existing homes ($c = 1$) and homes located outside the central county ($x = 1$) is negative and equally negligible ($R = 0.03$). Incomes are slightly lower outside the central county [the correlation between x and $ln(Y)$ is -0.19] and the down payment percentage is somewhat lower ($R = 0.29$).[7] It is important to note that the five correlation coefficients discussed would have been zero if every cell in the five-dimensional grid had been filled with at least 12 mortgages each and the dropout pattern did not reveal systematic differences in the frequency of mortgages in particular cells.

THE REGRESSION EQUATION

The four basic relationships discussed above can be utilized in explaining delinquency risk. The approach used is to regress the annual rates of delinquency for each cohort against the values for each of the four factors: (1) L/V ratio, (2) income of mortgagor, (3) location of mortgaged asset inside or outside the central county, and (4) relative age of the mortgaged asset, whether new or existing. The transformed values for the L/V ratio and the income of the mortgagor are given in table 5.1. In the absence of numerical values for the location factor and the relative age factor (new and existing), so-called "dummy factors" are utilized. A dummy factor (or variable) can be used when dealing with a dichotomous factor, that is, a factor that assumes one or two states at each point in time. For example, a location inside the central county is assigned a value of zero, and a location outside the central county is assigned a value of one. Similarly, a new house is assigned a value of zero, and an existing house a value of one. The total relationship used may be written out as

$$
\text{annual rate of delinquency in each cohort} = f \begin{bmatrix} (1) & \text{the relative age—new or existing} \\ (2) & \text{the location of the house—inside} \\ & \text{or outside central county} \\ (3) & \text{the equity-to-value ratio} = (1 - L/V) \\ (4) & \text{the annual income of the mortgagor.} \end{bmatrix} \quad \textbf{(5.1)}
$$

In the regression method, the delinquency rate is called the "dependent variable"; that is, its value is dependent upon the values that occur for the other four factors describing the cohort relationship at each point in time. The other four factors are called the "independent variables." It is presumed that the four factors are interrelated to some extent, and will therefore interact with each other. For example, a mortgagor with low income would normally have a low down payment, resulting in a high L/V ratio, and would very likely live in an existing house located in the center city within the central county. To capture this interactive effect that multiplies the number of relationships, a multiplicative form, as expressed by an exponential function, is used in the regression. A log transform is used to reduce the exponential relationships to a linear form.

THE BASIC REGRESSION RESULTS

With the logarithm of delinquency rates (D/M) as the dependent variable, the basic regression equation is the log transformation of

$$
100(D/M) = a_0 e^{a1c} e^{a2x} d e^{a4d2} [10(1 - L/V)]^{a5} (V/1{,}000)^{a6}. \quad \textbf{(5.2)}
$$

The equation containing all the variables used in the construction of the mortgage cohorts, except z, is reproduced in table 5.3.

Explanation of the Regression Results

In the new versus existing houses, mortgages on existing houses would appear to be 43 percent riskier with respect to delinquency than mortgages on new houses. In other words, when comparing mortgages on existing houses with mortgages on new houses, there is a 43 percent higher likelihood that a mortgage on an existing house will be delinquent than a mortgage on a new house. The 43 percent is obtained by adding the value of the intercept, 0.075, to the coefficient of new versus existing, 0.353, both values rounded to two places.

A house in a location outside the central county reduces the risk of delinquency substantially, by over 47 percent (47 percent = antilog $- 0.64025 = 0.527 - 1 = -0.472$). The minus sign indicates a decreasing effect. Since the central county in a standard metropolitan statistical area usually contains many high-income neighborhoods and subdivisions, the substantial reduction in delinquency risk from a location outside the central county may reflect the relatively high

Table 5.3
Regression Results for Annual Delinquency Rates

"New" vs. "Existing"	"Inside" vs. "Outside" Central County	Age of Mortgage		Equity-Value Ratio	Mortgagor Income
c	x	$l_n(d)$	d^2	$l_n 10(1 - L/V)$	$l_n(Y/1000)$
0.35303*	-0.64025**	0.31052**	-0.00858**	-0.76212**	-0.53292**
(2.49)	(-3.20)	(3.93)	(-2.82)	(7.63)	(-4.58)

Intercept = 0.07814, R^2 = .075, N = 1236, F-Value = 16.58.

The dependent variable is l_n (100 D/M).

Note: t values are given in parentheses. Coefficients significant at the 5% level are followed by *, those significant at the 1% level by **.

Table 5.4
**Risk Indexes for Separate Variations in Mortgage Age, Loan-to-Value Ratio, or
Income of Mortgagor**

(d) Age (Yrs)	Risk Index	(L/V) Loan Value (%)	Risk Index	(Y) Income ($)	Risk Index (%)
1	100	50	50	5,000	145
2	122	55	54	6,000	131
3	132	60	59	7,000	121
4	136	65	65	8,000	113
5	135	70	73	9,000	106
6	130	75	84	10,000	100
7	122	80	100	11,000	95
8	112	85	124	12,000	91
9	100	88	147	13,000	87
10	88	90	170	14,000	84
11	76	91	192	15,000	81
12	64	92	201	16,000	78
13	53	93	222	17,000	75
14	43	94	250	18,000	73
15	34	95	288	20,000	69

Note: The risk indexes are calculated from the regression in table 5.3,
the base in each case is underlined, and the risk index equals 100,
the coefficients for age, original loan-to-value ratio, and income
are extrapolated beyond the observed range by assuming stability
of the regression coefficients.

delinquency rates of the low-income neighborhoods in the inner city, which may dominate the lower-delinquency area within the county.

The age of the mortgage can be treated both as a level and as a squared term to obtain its special characteristics, because delinquency risk rises in the first few years and then subsides for the remainder of the life of the mortgage.

The negative sign of the equity-to-value ratio indicates that delinquency risk is reduced with rising equity-to-value ratio. The size of the equity-to-value ratio coefficient, -0.76212, indicates that delinquency rates will rise by over two-thirds if the equity-to-value ratio drops from 20 to 10 percent, which implies the loan-to-value ratio rising from 80 to 90 percent. Delinquency rates will jump another 70 percent, if the loan-to-value ratio rises further from 90 to 95 percent (equity-to-value ratio falls from 10 to 5 percent). This relationship is shown in table 5.4. Risk of delinquency and default increases significantly at loan-to-value ratios above 90 percent, which corresponds to equity-to-value ratios of less than 10 percent. Reactions by the mortgagor to perceived negative net equity in the home during times of income, domestic, or occupation difficulty leading to termination of employment may result in delinquency and/or default.

The income of the mortgagor has a negative relationship with delinquency risk, as shown by the negative sign of the coefficient in the last column of table 5.3. For example, delinquency rates in any cohort would decrease by 45 percent if family income increased from $5,000 to $10,000.

COHORT ANALYSIS USING RISK INDEXES

Indexes of the risks that may be contributed by each of the three factors are presented in table 5.4. The risk indexes are calculated from the values of the coefficients of the factors in table 5.3. The index numbers of delinquency rates are ratios calculated for given ranges of values for the independent variables relative to the calculated value of the base. The values of the coefficients for the three variables are then extrapolated beyond the range of values observed in the data by assuming that the values computed for the factors shown in table 5.3 would not be affected by the data not observed.

For the age of the mortgage, the index is set equal to 100 in year 1 and rises to 122 in the second year. This means that in a cohort where delinquency rates are set equal to 100 in year 1, those rates would be expected to be 22 percent higher in year 2. The peak of the annual delinquency rates occurs at age 4 at 136, after which the rates fall to 34 at age 15, which is approximately one-third of the 100 set in the first year. This shows that delinquency risk increases in the early years of the mortgage and reaches a peak at about the fourth year, after which it falls continuously.

The risk index for the loan-to-value ratio is calculated by using the median loan-to-value ratio, or the ratio closest to the median, as the base for comparison and setting it equal to 100. As expected, if the loan-to-value ratio is raised above 90 percent, delinquency risk is increased significantly.

The risk index for income of the mortgagor is constructed by setting the median income of $10,000 equal to 100 and computing the index for a range of values, as shown in the sixth column of table 5.4. As expected, delinquency risk is highest in the lower income range and declines as income rises. For example, in any cohort, a rise in family income from $5,000 to $10,000 will lower the delinquency rate by about 45 percent.

Cohort Comparison for Relative Riskiness

The risk indexes in table 5.4 are used to compare the relative riskiness of blocks of mortgages in different cohorts.

Example 5.3. Assume two blocks of mortgages of equal age located within the central county with the following mortgagor incomes and loan-to-value ratios:

	Block 1	Block 2
Mortgagor income	$8,000	$12,000
Loan-to-value ratio	90 percent	75 percent

Step 1. To compute the relative riskiness, index numbers from table 5.4 are assigned for the incomes and loan-to-value ratios given above:

	Risk Index	
	Block 1	Block 2
Mortgagor income	113 percent	91 percent
Loan-to-value ratio	170 percent	84 percent

The indexes are treated as percentages, since they were computed on a base of 100. Next, a composite index for each block is obtained by multiplying the index for income and loan-to-value ratio.

Step 2.

composite index = mortgagor income index × loan-to-value index,

$$CI_1 = \frac{113 \times 170}{100} = \frac{19,210}{100} = 192.10,$$

$$CI_2 = \frac{91 \times 84}{100} = \frac{7,644}{100} = 76.44.$$

In comparison, the composite risk for block 1, 192.10, is greater than the composite index for block 2, 76.44.

Table 5.5
Deviation of the Lower- and Upper-Bound Coefficients

	Coefficient	t Value	Standard Deviations Coefficient/ t-Value	90% Confidence Factor 1.28 x (2)	Lower Bound (1) − (3)	Upper Bound (1) + (4)
	(1)	(2)	(3)	(4)	(5)	(6)
Equity-value	−0.7621	7.63	−0.0999	−0.1279	−0.6342	−0.8900
Income	−0.5329	4.58	−0.1164	−0.1489	−0.3840	−0.6818

The risk indexes in table 5.4 are recalculated using the lower-bound values for the coefficients in column 5. Following steps 1 to 3 above, the relative index is computed for the lower bound. The relative index for the upper-bound values of the coefficients in column 6 is computed in the same way. One can therefore assume with 90% confidence that each of the "true coefficients" will not be smaller in absolute size than the lower-bound values or greater in absolute size than the upper-bound values obtained here.

Step 3.

$$\text{relative index} = \frac{\text{block 1 composite index}}{\text{block 2 composite index}}$$

$$= \frac{192.10}{76.44} = 2.51.$$

This indicates that block 1 is 2.51 times as risky as block 2. Therefore, in any given year or holding period, for mortgages of the same age, the expected delinquency rates of block 1 would be 151 percent higher than the expected delinquency rates of block 2.

Confidence in Relative Index

How much confidence can be placed in the estimate of the relative index computed above? A determination can be made by constructing a statistical confidence interval and checking to see if the relative index falls within it. The lower- and upper-bound coefficient values are computed in table 5.5. The coefficients and *t* values are obtained from table 5.3.

Relative Index

Lower bound	2.09
Upper bound	2.98

This shows that at the lower bound, the first block is at least 2.09 times as risky as the second block. At the upper bound, the first block is no more than 2.98 times as risky as the second block. The confidence interval is given as

confidence interval = 2.09 to 2.98.

The relative index of 2.51 falls within the 90 percent confidence interval, and it is therefore valid to conclude that statistically the first block of mortgages is around two and one-half times as risky as the second group of mortgages. The confidence interval of the relative index can be a very useful tool in the hands of loan officers, bank examiners, and portfolio managers when examining the differences in delinquency risk among cohorts of mortgage loans. Cohort analysis can be effectively used to measure the relative riskiness of different groups of mortgage loans packaged for sale in the secondary mortgage market.

NOTES

1. Dorothy S. Projector and Gertrude S. Weiss, *Surveyor of Financial Characteristics of Consumers* (Washington, D.C.: Board of Governors of the Federal Reserve System, 1966), p. 110.

2. The FHA found that "the highest proportion of acquisitions (foreclosures) to total cases insured was for properties approved prior to the start of construction. Since seven-eighths of new construction commitments are issued to builders, this experience is specifically applicable to mortgage risks associated with speculative construction." U.S. Congress, Senate, Hearings Before a Subcommittee of the Senate Committee on Banking and Currency, *FHA Mortgage Foreclosures,* 88th Cong., 2nd sess., 1964, p. 254.

3. Mortgages that are delinquent for more than 40 days are classified as delinquent. For example, delinquency is registered if a payment due on June 1 has not been paid by July 10, and only first delinquencies are recorded on any mortgage.

4. The total number of mortgages originated by the lending institution between 19X0 and 19Y2 was 15,461. All observations with information missing on any of the variables used in this analysis, or signifying out-of-state mortgages or mortgages other than those for single-family homes, were discarded. As a result, the sample contains only about one-half of the population of mortgages. It is not clear what biases, if any, were introduced by eliminating the items with incomplete information. As the lender's efforts to obtain complete information were especially directed at borrowers constituting marginal credit risks, then the aggregate delinquency rate in the sample would overstate expected delinquencies in the population. There is no reason, however, to assume that any of our structural coefficients will be biased since cohort analysis is insensitive of the logarithms of delinquency rates on the assumption that the latter are log-normally distributed.

5. For example, with 10 mortgages in a cohort and no delinquencies on them in a year, the measured delinquency rate is 0.1 percent. With one delinquency, it would jump to 10 percent and with two to 20 percent. In either event, the measured rates would inevitably deviate significantly from the mean of 1.15 percent because of the choppiness introduced by dividing by small numbers.

6. FHA-insured mortgages. See George M. von Furstenberg, "Risk Structures and the Distribution of Benefits Within the FHA Mortgage Insurance Program," *Journal of Money, Credit and Banking* 2 (1970): 303–22.

7. The loan-to-value ratio has a tendency to decline in periods of credit tightness. For instance, for conventional mortgages originated by savings and loans of new (existing) homes, it fell from 76.0 (75.3) percent in 1968 to 74.2 (73.5) percent in 1970. Up to the mid-1960s, however, loan-to-value ratios had shown a persistent tendency to rise. See *Federal Home Loan Bank Board Journal* 5 (1972): 33. Theoretical analyses of this cyclical relationship have been provided by Richard F. Muth, "Interest Rates, Contract Terms, and the Allocation of Mortgage Funds," *Journal of Finance* 17 (1962): 63–80; Allen F. Jung, "Terms on Conventional Mortgage Loans on Existing Homes," *Journal of Finance* 17 (1962): 432–43; and Alfred N. Page, "The Variation of Mortgage Interest Rates," *Journal of Business* 37 (1964): 280–94.

CHAPTER 6

Discriminant Function Analysis Classification

In this chapter, a discriminant function analysis is presented and then used to identify those characteristics that contribute to mortgage foreclosure. Discriminant analysis is most suitable for use when the dependent factor (or variable) consists of discrete, a priori groups and produces an index that allows classification of an observation into one of these groups. To avoid the problems that arise in scaling data, no assumptions are made about the intervals between the groups in the discriminant function. Direct comparison of two or more groups can be made at the same time, and differences between the groups and a set of discriminating factors can be studied. Discriminant analysis treats the dependent factor as being measured at the nominal level (i.e., in groups); therefore, neither the group categories nor the discriminating factors are defined as the dependent or the independent factor.

THE CANONICAL DISCRIMINANT FUNCTION

Three basic steps are involved in the discriminant analysis process: (1) Identify group categories that are mutually exclusive such that each group can be separately identified by a probability distribution of its own attributes, (2) tabulate data for each of the groups, and (3) derive linear combinations of the characteristics that minimize the probability of misclassification, which gives the best discriminating power.

Examples of mortgage groups that are mutually exclusive are good and foreclosed loans or good and delinquent loans. A loan cannot be good (current) and foreclosed at the same time. Suppose we want to use two ratios, X_1 and X_2, to discriminate between the two groups of loans: good (g) and foreclosed (f). Let X_1 represent the loan-to-value ratio and X_2 represent the payment-to-income ratio. Using the above relationships, a canonical discriminant function is represented in the following formulation:

Figure 6.1
Z Score Distributions

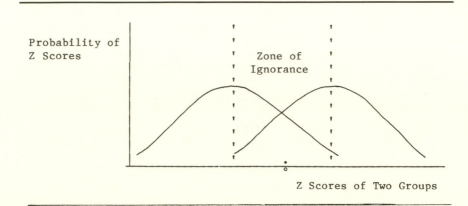

Probability of
Z Scores

Zone of
Ignorance

Z Scores of Two Groups

$$Z = u_1 X_1 + u_2 X_2, \tag{6.1}$$

which is a linear combination of the discriminating factors X_1, the loan-to-value ratio, and X_2, the payment-to-income ratio. It is possible to combine X_1 and X_2 linearly in such a way that the sum of the products with their respective coefficients, u_1 and u_2, produces an index value (Z) that is useful in discriminating among members of the two groups. The discriminating power of the two factors X_1 and X_2 depends upon the values of the means and standard deviations of their respective probability distributions. Since the means of X_1 and X_2 are different, that is, $u_1 \neq u_2$, the size of the standard deviation of each factor will determine the discriminating power of the function, as in the following examples:

> *Case 6.1.* If the standard deviations of each factor X_1 and X_2 are relatively small and do not overlap, the discriminating power of Z will be high.

> *Case 6.2.* If the standard deviations of X_1 and X_2 are very large and they overlap over a portion of the distribution, there is a greater chance of error in classifying observations that fall in the region of overlap. The region of overlap is called the "zone of ignorance," shown in figure 6.1.

CLASSIFICATION MATRIX

Table 6.1 presents a classification matrix that shows how a discriminant analysis can help in the classification of mortgagors. In the case of the two groups "default" and "not default," the mortgagor would belong to either one of the two a priori groups, which is also classified as the "actual group membership."

Table 6.1
The Classification Matrix

Actual Group Membership	Predicted Group Membership	
	ND	D
ND	C_1	I_1
D	I_2	C_2

For example, the actual group membership of a mortgagor who did not default over the life of the loan is not default (ND) and for one that defaulted is default (D). The objective is to build a discriminant model that can predict the outcome of each case correctly with minimum error in the predicted group membership. The initials C and I are used to represent correct and incorrect predictions, respectively, by the model. C_1 indicates that a mortgagor whose payment performance, or loan-servicing performance, is good over the life of the loan is correctly classified as not default, and C_2 shows that a mortgagor who defaults is correctly classified as such. I_1 and I_2 indicate incorrect classifications: I_1 represents good mortgagors incorrectly classified as default, and I_2 shows default incorrectly classified as not default. Both I_1 and I_2 should be zero if all classifications are correct. Because it is difficult to classify every mortgagor correctly, the objective here is to minimize the number of incorrect classifications.

STEPWISE DISCRIMINANT FUNCTION ANALYSIS

In constructing a canonical discriminant function model, the objective is to select factors that will minimize misclassification in the model. The computed values of Z for the two groups should be as far apart as possible to eliminate the possibility of overlap in their standard deviations. Factors selected are entered in the discriminant function one at a time in the descending order of their contribution. This approach, known as "stepwise discriminant function analysis," permits the inclusion of factors with the highest *F* value being "partialed" against variables already included.

The Factors

Twelve factors are used in the canonical discriminant function to represent loan, borrower, property, and lender characteristics. The factors include loan-to-value ratio, annual payment-to-annual income, loan insurance, marital status, profession, number of dependents, borrower's age, type of property, original maturity of mortgage, and other debt payments. Some of the factors are divided into intervals to reflect their input on mortgage risk. The purpose of the loan is broken down into purchase, construction, repair and remodeling, and refinancing. The borrower's age is divided into five-year intervals: 18 to 24 years, 25 to 29 years, 30 to 34 years, 35 to 39 years, 40 to 44 years, 45 to 49 years, 50 to 54 years, and 60 years and over. Seven professional groups are used for borrower's profession: self-employed, salesman, clerical, unskilled labor, professional, skilled labor, and service, etc. The number of dependents tells how many dependents the borrower has, from one to five plus. The type of property factor indicates whether it is a one-, two-, or three-family property.

The 12 factors are classified into quantitative and qualitative types. The quantitative factors have numerical values: the L/V ratio, annual payment-to-annual income ratio, and original maturity of the loan. The qualitative factors are transformed into so-called "dummy factors" through the assignment of dummy values of zero and one. The assignment of quantitative dummy values to the qualitative factors permits their incorporation in the canonical discriminant function. The qualitative factors that are assigned dummy values are presence of FHA or VA insurance, presence of other debt payments, type of employment, and purpose of the loan. Qualitative factors that represent various categories are subdivided in order to identify each borrower's category and to examine more closely how the various intervals of these factors impact on mortgage risk. As an example, the factor of purpose of the loan can be for purchase of a house, construction, repair and remodeling, or refinancing. For each loan, one or more of these categories may be applicable and will be identified as such. A quantitative factor that covers a range of values is similarly divided into preselected intervals to identify the interval associated with the borrower.

A Priori Groups

The initial step in discriminant analysis is the identification of the a priori groups to be studied. The groupings used in this mortgage analysis are the two loan payment statuses not default and default. It is important that the a priori groups be mutually exclusive to minimize the possibility of misclassification. A loan that has defaulted and is under foreclosure proceedings, or one that has been foreclosed, is separate and distinct from a loan that has not defaulted.

DATA AND DATA COLLECTION

Data for the canonical discriminant analysis are obtained from the borrower's application in the loan files where information on most of the factors is requested. Consequently, loans with incomplete information on any factor cannot be included in the data set. Only loans with a full data set of information on all the variables can be used since data on every factor on each loan are required.

Data are collected for each of the a priori groups: current and default. When the available number of mortgage loans is large, a stratified simple random sampling may be taken to obtain an unbiased sample of loans for the analysis.

Because the number of foreclosed loans is usually held to a minimum by the lender, there may be just enough foreclosed mortgaged loans to do the analysis, and no random sampling can be done.

Original and Holdout Sample

A 20 percent holdout sample is taken through systematic random sampling of each a priori group from the complete set of data collected. The original sample is used to derive the discriminant function, and the holdout sample is used to test the predictive ability of the model developed of the canonical discriminant function. It is important to ensure that the ability of the discriminant model obtained is not limited to the original data from which it is developed. It is necessary, therefore, to test the model on a totally different set of data; hence, the holdout sample. The predictive ability of the model will be somewhat lower in the holdout sample but not significantly different from the results of the original sample. For example, if the predictive ability of the discriminant function on the original sample is 70 percent, it is to be expected that the prediction on the holdout sample should be slightly less, for example, 60 to 65 percent. If, on the other hand, the predictive ability of the model on the holdout sample is only 35 percent, then the model's capacity to predict will not be as valid.

Correlation Between Variables

It is useful to obtain a correlation matrix of the factors to be used in the canonical discriminant function to show the degree of correlation between the factors. Low correlation between the independent factors is an indication that the factors are to some extent independent of one another. On the other hand, high correlations between the independent factors would indicate that the problem of multicollinearity could significantly affect how meaningful the coefficients of the canonical discriminant function are.

Three basic assumptions are required when discriminant analysis is used: (1) No factor may be a linear combination of other discriminating factors. This requires that neither the sum nor the average of several factors can be used at the same time. (2) The population covariance matrices are equal for each group. This assumption permits simplification of the procedure to calculate the discriminant function and of some of the tests of the significance of the analysis results. (3) Each group is drawn from a population that has a multivariate normal distribution. This requirement permits the computation of tests of significance and probabilities of group membership to be precise.

THE CANONICAL DISCRIMINANT CLASSIFICATION FUNCTION

The assigned data are used to derive the canonical discriminant classification function in a two-step approach. First, the number of independent factors is reduced in a stepwise manner to a select group of factors found to be the best in discriminating between the two groups of mortgage payment status categories. Second, the select group of factors obtained from the stepwise process is used to form linear predictive models.

The Stepwise Canonical Discriminant Analysis

A stepwise discriminant function approach is used to identify the factors that best discriminate between the two mortgage payment status groups. Factors are entered in a decreasing order of importance in the discriminant analysis on the basis of their contribution in explaining the variance among the mortgage payment status groups. As each new factor is added to the discriminant group, a test is made of the level of significance using the F statistic of the contribution of each factor in the group in explaining the variance. When a factor's contribution to explaining the variance falls below the level of significance determined by the F statistic, the factor is dropped from the discriminant analysis. The stepwise process of adding and removing factors continues until all 12 factors identified above have gone through the discriminant analysis, and the factors with the

Table 6.2
Important Factors in Distinguishing A Priori Groups*

	Discriminant Classification Function	
Factor	Not Default	Default
Property type: 3 family	0.61245	2.90254
Junior Financing	2.26217	4.63980
Dependents: 5 or more	1.18123	2.32477
Loan/value	25.86931	28.15684
Entrepreneur	2.82319	3.60174
Salesman	2.69871	3.98632
Other debts	3.16347	4.54231
Dependents: 4	3.13396	3.89517
Dependents: none	1.39351	2.14975
Constant term	−12.04645	−15.15178

* Factors listed by sequence entered in the canonical discriminant function.

highest level of contribution, as determined from the F statistic test, are identified. The nine factors with the highest level of contribution in explaining the variance are presented in table 6.2.

Classification Procedure

To classify a mortgage loan in one of the two payment status groups, current or default, the value of each of the nine factors listed in table 6.2 for each loan is multiplied by the factor's coefficient, and their products summed up for each of the two groups. The loan is classified under the group with the higher total value of summed products plus the constant term.

Classification Rule: Classify a mortgage loan under the a priori group with the highest total value of the summed products plus the constant term.

From the classification procedure, the following points are worth noting about the coefficients: (1) Positive values of the coefficients increase the total value of the summed products, while negative coefficients reduce the total value. (2) The likelihood of a loan being classified in the group increases with the inclusion of coefficients with high positive values. (3) Similarly, the likelihood of loan classification in a group is reduced when it includes coefficients with lower or negative values.

The Canonical Discriminant Function

A canonical discriminant function is formed by a linear combination of the significant factors from the stepwise discriminant analysis presented in table 6.2. The factors are presented in the order in which they are entered:

$$Z = a_1 \text{ property (three family)} + a_2 \text{ junior financing} + a_3 \text{ dependents (five or more)} + a_4 \text{ L/V ratio} + a_5 \text{ entrepreneur} + a_6 \text{ salesman} + a_7 \text{ other debts owned} + a_8 \text{ dependents (4)} + a_9 \text{ no dependents (4)} + a_0.$$

The canonical discriminant function embodies a combination of statistically significant factors that produces the greatest distance between the mean values of the default and not default groups.

The two columns shown in table 6.2 present coefficients representing the two canonical discriminant functions for default and not default groups. The coefficients in the default group are larger than those in the not default group, indicating that each of the factors has a greater likelihood to distinguish mortgage loans prone to default risk than otherwise.

For the first factor, three-family property, the default coefficient is almost six times the size of the not default coefficient, an indication that mortgage loans for three-family properties are highly prone to default. A probable reason for the tendency of three-family properties to default is that this type of property is usually a single-family residence subdivided into three apartments and owned by small entrepreneurs with meager financial resources. Two related causes lead to abandonment and default. The first is that in order to minimize their risk exposure, these owners try to get the quickest payback and in the process carry out little or no maintenance, which results in dilapidation and the equity built up in the property diminishes, and may decline to the point of abandonment. A second reason is a situation in which neighborhood property prices are declining and it is to the owner's advantage to abandon the property rather than incur additional out-of-pocket loss when the selling price is less than the payout balance.

The default coefficients for the second and third factors are more than twice the size of the coefficient of the not default factors. Junior financing has always been associated with increased risk in a mortgage loan. Before its recent popularity, junior financing was associated with borrowers who were seen to be in some degree of financial difficulty and had to assume additional financial leverage. The higher rate of interest on junior financing is also an indication of the premium required for the increased risk. The higher debt service required when junior financing is present creates an added financial burden in the mortgagor's budget in times of crisis or financial distress. With inadequate resources to meet the higher debt service during financial exigencies, there is a greater likelihood that a mortgagor with junior financing will default.

The default coefficients of the factor of five or more dependents is about two times the size of the not default coefficient, which indicates that a borrower having a large family with five or more dependents is more likely to default than keep the loan current. The reason for the increased risk would seem apparent. Because of the high cost of maintaining a large family, during financial exigencies a mortgagor with minimal financial resources is apt to default.

The loan-to-value ratio has the highest coefficients of 28.15684 for default and 25.86931 for not default. The high coefficient value reflects two things: (1) the importance of the loan-to-value ratio factor and (2) the very small size of the value of the factor. Recall that the contribution of the factor is the product of its value multiplied by the value of the coefficient. Given the small size of the factor expressed as a fraction, the higher the size of the coefficient, the larger the product and the greater the significance of the factor. Since the loan-to-value ratio represents the relative proportion of the loan to the value of the underlying property, the higher the loan-to-value ratio, the lower is the residual equity-to-value ratio. The product of a fractional loan-to-value ratio with a high coefficient value results in a high contribution value for this factor, showing its significance as an important risk indicator. A reason for the importance of the loan-to-value ratio factor in default risk can be gleaned from its reciprocal, the equity-to-value ratio. A low equity-to-value ratio indicates the borrower's equity in the property is commensurately low. In declining neighborhoods and in deflationary environments, if the property value falls, the loan-to-value ratio rises and the equity-to-value ratio falls. When equity values are very low or negative, the borrower can minimize out-of-pocket expenses by defaulting.

The next two factors in table 6.2 represent two categories of borrower employment, an important indicator in mortgage risk. Some employment categories exhibit more stability than others. Mortgagors in stable employment have a more stable income stream and are in a better position to service their mortgage regularly and punctually. Since the coefficient for salesman of 3.98632 is higher than the coefficient for self-employed of 3.60174, a salesman is considered a greater foreclosure risk than a self-employed person. Only two of the seven employment profession categories turned up as significant factors in default risk. The other five professions exhibited relatively smaller likelihood of foreclosure risk.

The factor of four dependents is also shown as significant. A family of five (borrower with four dependents) is a marginally large family, and the previous discussion on five or more dependents applies equally as well. Another factor that is significant for default risk is a mortgagor with no dependents.

PREDICTIVE ABILITY OF THE DISCRIMINANT FUNCTON

As indicated above, the primary objective in building the canonical discriminant function is to develop a predictive model with the capacity to discriminate between potential borrowers who are a good credit risk and those with a higher likelihood of default risk. The predictive ability of the discriminant function is embodied in its classification function, which is used to classify the mortgagors into one of the two a priori groups, not default and default.

The predictive ability of the classification function is tested on both the original and the holdout samples. The classification matrix on the original sample presented in table 6.3 shows that 76 percent of mortgagors whose actual group membership is not default are correctly classified, with 24 percent of that group

Table 6.3
Classification Matrix: Original Sample

Actual Group Membership	Predicted Group Membership			
	Not Default		Default	
	No.	Percentage	No.	Percentage
Not default	342	76	108	24
Default	40	36	71	64

Table 6.4
Classification Matrix: Holdout Sample

	Predicted Group Membership			
	Not Default		Default	
Actual Group Membership	No.	Percentage	No.	Percentage
Not Default	79	72	31	28
Default	9	32	19	68

incorrectly classified. Of the default membership group, 64 percent are correctly classified, leaving 36 percent incorrectly classified.

The classification function did a slightly better job in discriminating within the not foreclosed than within the default actual group membership. The incorrect classification in each actual group membership falls in the zone of ignorance depicted in figure 6.1, where the Z function for the two groups overlaps. Overall, 74 percent are correctly classified.

To test whether or not the predictive ability of the canonical discriminant function obtained in table 6.2 is limited to the original sample from which it was derived, its predictive ability is also tested on the holdout sample. The classification matrix on the holdout sample presented in table 6.4 shows that in the not default actual group membership, 72 percent are correctly classified, leaving 28 percent incorrectly classified. In comparison with the original sample classification, there is a 4 percent drop in the percentage correctly classified for the default group actual membership in the original sample in table 6.3. For the two a priori groups in table 6.4, 72 percent of the actual group membership are correctly classified.

The canonical discriminant model presented in table 6.2 is shown to have significant ability to predict foreclosure risk.

CHAPTER 7

Risk Indexes

AN INDEX OF LOAN QUALITY

The preceding empirical analysis has produced a number of estimated regression equations of the form

$$y_t = b_0 + b_1 x_{1t} + \ldots + b_n x_{nt}. \tag{7.1}$$

The values $b_1, \ldots, b_n$ are the estimated coefficients of the n explanatory factors $x_{1t}, \ldots, x_{nt}$. The factors $X_{1t}, \ldots, X_{nt}$ represent the observed values of the loan, borrower, property, and neighborhood characteristics for the tth loan. Substituting in equation (7.1) the observed values of $x_{1t}, \ldots, x_{nt}$ for a particular loan, a value, y_t, is obtained that is the predicted value of $\hat{y}_t$. The value of y_t is either zero or one, with zero indicating a good loan.

If equation (7.1) were a perfectly accurate predictive equation, the computed value $\hat{y}_t$ and the actual value y_t would be equal for every mortgage. In every case, the predicted value would equal the observed value; there would be no errors or disparities in the results. Equation (7.1) would then be an ideal predictive equation. Unfortunately, this is not the case, a fact highlighted by the R^2 being less than one.

The quality predictions generated by a sample of mortgages will typically range from zero to one, with a few lying outside of this interval. Recall that in each regression, a "good" loan is given the value of zero, a loan of poor quality the value of one. Consequently, the prediction quality of a given mortgage, $\hat{y}_t$, may be viewed as an *index of loan quality*. The closer a mortgage's index is to zero, the higher is the indicated quality of the mortgage. Mortgages with indexes close to one would tend to be inferior to those with indexes substantially below one.

To construct risk indexes, the regressions reported in table 4.1 and reproduced

Table 7.1

Coefficients and *F* Ratios of Explanatory Variables in Default Risk

Variable	Coefficient	F Ratio
Loan—to—loan value:		
Over 90%	0.08235*	16.75
85 – 90%	0.04421	2.46
Payment to income:		
Over 30%	0.09180*	7.80
22 – 30%	-0.02703	1.49
Age of mortgagor:		
Over 50	0.04465*	3.24
Less than 30	-0.02609	2.32
Number of years with employer	-0.00367*	15.76
Age of property	0.00049	1.57
Junior financing	0.19653*	13.75
Unemployment rate	0.60069*	4.50
Per capita changes in crimes against property	-0.34399	0.34
VA insurance	0.00128	0.00
FHA insurance	-0.09032*	12.26
Price of property	-0.00279*	15.52
Number of children	0.00695	2.38
Refinanced loan	0.06178*	4.55
Term of loan	-0.00030	0.06
Monthly income	-0.00118	0.01
Multifamily unit	-0.02018	0.46
Private insurance	-0.03497	1.67
FHA-235 loan	-0.06886	1.25

*Statistically significant at the .95 level.

Source: Regression Analysis

in table 7.1 are used. For each good or foreclosed loan, the observed values of the explanatory factors are substituted into equation (7.1) using the coefficients $b_0, \ldots, b_n$ of the regression reported in table 7.1. Thus, for each good or foreclosed loan, the value y_t is calculated, which is the value of y_t predicted by the regression equation.

RISK INDEX FOR GOOD VERSUS FORECLOSED LOANS

Using the regression equations in table 7.1 for good versus foreclosed loans, the value of y_t is calculated for each sample loan, both good and foreclosed, and

Table 7.2
Good Versus Foreclosed: Sample Data

(1)	(2)	(3)	(4)	(5)	(6)
Values of y_t	Number Good	Number Foreclosed	Total	Relative Frequency of Total	Cumulative Frequency of Total
less than .05	67	1	68	.044	.044
.05 - .10	250	6	256	.167	.212
.10 - .15	404	17	421	.275	.487
.15 - .20	353	20	373	.244	.731
.20 - .25	187	23	210	.137	.868
.25 - .30	86	23	109	.071	.940
.30 - .35	33	16	49	.032	.972
.35 - .40	17	8	25	.016	.988
.40 - .45	4	7	11	.007	.995
.45 - .50	3	2	5	.003	.998
.50 - .55	0	0	0	.000	.998
.55 - .60	0	1	1	.001	.999
.60 - .65	1	0	1	.001	1.000

Source: Table 7.1.

the values of y_t are grouped according to the intervals (less than 0.05), (0.05, 0.09), (0.10, 0.14), . . . , (over 0.95).

The distribution of values of y_t so obtained is given in table 7.2. To interpret this table, note, for example, that 24.4 percent of the loans in this sample have values of y_t in the range of 0.15 to 0.19, while 73.1 percent have y_t values below 0.19.

The observed relative frequencies reported in table 7.2 cannot as yet be interpreted as probabilities because while the sample includes every foreclosed loan, only a small sample of the good loans is used. Thus, foreclosures are proportionately overrepresented, making it appear as though they occur much

Table 7.3
Good Versus Foreclosed: Projected Population Data

(1)	(2)	(3)	(4)	(5)	(6)
Values of y_t	Number Good	Number Foreclosed	Good and Foreclosed	Relative Frequency of Good & Foreclosed	Cumulative Frequency of Good & Foreclosed
less than .05	1340	1	1341	.0475	.0475
.05 - .10	5000	6	5006	.1774	.2256
.10 - .15	8080	17	8097	.2869	.5125
.15 - .20	7060	20	7080	.2509	.7634
.20 - .25	3740	23	3763	.1333	.8967
.25 - .30	1720	23	1743	.0618	.9585
.30 - .35	660	16	676	.0240	.9825
.35 - .40	340	8	348	.0120	.9945
.45 - .50	80	7	87	.0030	.9975
.50 - .55	0	0	0	.0000	.9995
.55 - .60	0	1	1	.0000	.9995
.60 - .65	20	0	20	.0005	1.0000

Source: Table 7.2

more frequently than they actually do; that is, the figures in the fifth column are too high for representing the probability of default for a loan taken at random from a lender's portfolio. The frequencies in column 5 of table 7.2 must be adjusted before the relative frequencies can be interpreted as default probabilities.

Good loans were sampled at random in the ratio of approximately 1 in 20, or 5 percent. Since the sample was representative of the institution's portfolio of good loans, on the average, 20 times as many good loans with values of y_t in each interval would be obtained.

Multiplying the number of good loans by 20 in each interval of column 2 in table 7.2 produces a more accurate picture of the true proportions of good loans in each interval, as presented in table 7.3.

If the regression equations are useful for predicting the quality of a given loan taken at random from an association's portfolio, it should be the case that good loans will have low values of y_t and foreclosures high values. The data in table 7.3 indicate that this is precisely the case.

In column 2 of table 7.3, the expected number of good loans per class interval is given for the entire population. Column 4 contains the total loans by intervals we would have expected to find in the entire loan portfolio, while column 6 gives the cumulative frequency distribution of values of y_t projected for the entire portfolio. As expected, most of the loans were good loans and most had y_t values close to zero.

The discriminating ability of the regression equation can be studied in a more refined way. From the bottom of column 2 of table 7.4, there are a total of 124 foreclosures. Columns 4 and 6 present the relative and cumulative frequency distributions, respectively, of these foreclosures. For example, from column 4, 16.1 percent of all 124 foreclosures had values of y_t between 0.15 and 0.19. From column 6, 35.5 percent of all foreclosures had y_t values below 0.19.

A plot of the data in column 6 of table 7.1 against that of column 5 of table 7.3 on a graph produces the curve in figure 7.1. If the regression equation has low discriminating power, the curve will lie near the 45-degree line. This would indicate, for example, that 30 percent of the foreclosures have y_t values in the lowest 30 percent of all loans, 50 percent of the foreclosures have y_t values in the lowest 50 percent of all loans, etc. On the other hand, if the equation has high discriminating power, it should produce a curve with a deep bow in it, so that much of the curve lies near the horizontal axis. In this case, for example, only 10 or 15 percent of the foreclosures might have values of y_t in the lowest 50 percent of all loans, indicating that few of the foreclosures have relatively low values of y_t.

Figure 7.1 indicates that the regression equation for good versus foreclosed loans has relatively good discriminating power. The points on the graph indicate that if the loans are arranged according to their y_t values, only 19 percent of the foreclosures have y_t values in the lower 50 percent of the loans. Furthermore,

Table 7.4
Good Versus Foreclosed: Probability Index

(1) Values of y_t	(2) Number Foreclosed	(3) Good and Foreclosed	(4) Relative Frequency of Foreclosure Foreclosed/ Total Foreclosed	(5) Cumulative Frequency of Foreclosure	(6) Probability of Foreclosure Foreclosed/Good and Foreclosed
less than .05	1	1341	.009	.009	.00075
.05 – .10	6	5006	.048	.057	.00115
.10 – .15	17	8097	.137	.194	.00200
.15 – .20	20	7080	.161	.355	.00270
.20 – .25	23	3763	.185	.540	.00550
.25 – .30	23	1743	.185	.725	.01055
.30 – .35	16	676	.129	.854	.01635
.35 – .40	8	348	.065	.919	.01600
.40 – .45	7	87	.056	.975	.03180
.45 – .50	2	62	.016	.991	.02000
.50 – .55	0	0	.000	.991	
.55 – .60	1	1	.009	1.000	
.60 – .65	0	20	.000	1.000	
	124				

Figure 7.1
Good Versus Foreclosed

% of foreclosed loans

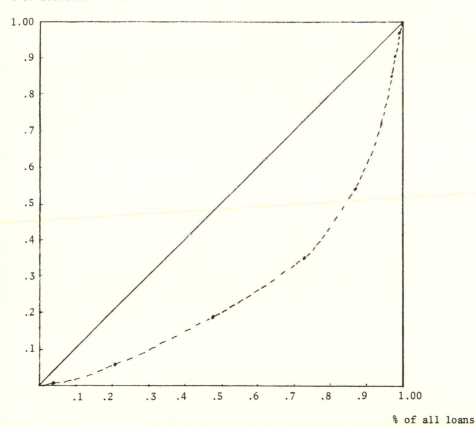

% of all loans

nearly 50 percent of the foreclosed loans have y_t values in the highest 20 percent of all values of y_t. It is the case that the equation assigns high values to foreclosed loans and low values to good loans, as was desired.

The data in table 7.4 can be used to construct a risk index measuring the probability that a loan, given its risk characteristics, will be foreclosed. From columns 2 and 3, we see that for the entire portfolio, we could expect 1,341 loans to have y_t values below 0.05, only 1 of which is a foreclosure. Of the loans with y_t values below 0.05, therefore, only 1 of 1,341, or 0.075 percent, were foreclosures. The value of 0.075 percent is interpreted as the percentage chance that a loan with a y_t value below 0.05 is a foreclosure. Finally, expressed in terms of

Figure 7.2
Probability Index

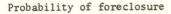

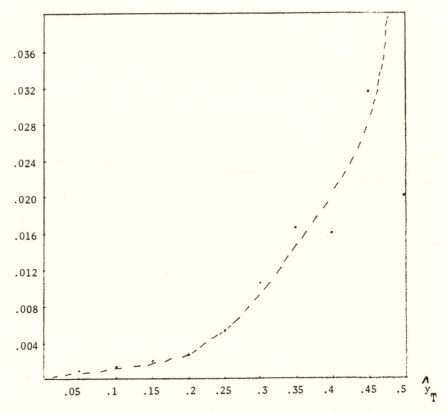

probabilities, we would say that a loan with a y_t value below 0.05 has a probability of 0.00075, that is, 0.075/100, of being foreclosed.

Similarly, in table 7.4, only 6 foreclosures were among the 5,006 loans having
y_t values in the interval 0.05 to 0.09. Column 6 of table 7.4 indicates that 0.115
percent of all loans with y_t values in the interval 0.05 to 0.09 were foreclosures.
Thus, if a loan has a y_t value in the interval 0.05 to 0.09, the probability of
foreclosure is 0.00115.

Column 6 of table 7.4 yields a set of values that can be used to predict the
probability of foreclosure for a loan having any specific value of y_t, that is, for a
given set of risk characteristics. For example, in figure 7.2 is presented a graph
of the probability index provided by column 6 of table 7.4 against y_t. Using the
graph (or the data in column 6), it can be assessed, for example, that if a loan had

a computed value of y_t of about 0.25, its probability of foreclosure would be approximately 0.00550.

Using the index, the probability of foreclosure for any loan can be determined, given the data concerning the particular loan characteristics. Given the values of $x_1, x_2, \ldots, x_n$ (where $x_1, x_2, \ldots, x_n$ represent the individual's age, number of children, etc.), these values can be substituted into the regression equation

$$y = b_0 + b_1x_1 + \ldots + b_nx_n,$$

where the values of $b_0, b_1, \ldots, b_n$ are obtained from table 7.1. Using the calculated value of y and column 6 of table 7.3, one can obtain the probability that the particular loan will be a foreclosure.

In addition, suppose the probability of foreclosure is computed for every loan in a portfolio. If the loan value of each such loan is weighted by its probability of foreclosure, we could obtain an index number measuring, in a sense, the overall quality of a portfolio. In this way, it would be possible to compare the portfolio quality of one association with that of another or to examine how an association's portfolio is changing over time.

RISK INDEX FOR GOOD VERSUS DELINQUENT LOANS

The process of developing a risk index for good versus foreclosed regressions described above is repeated here for the good versus delinquent regressions.

For each good or delinquent loan in the sample, the value of y_t is calculated using, as an example, the regression equation for good versus delinquent reported in table 7.5.

The indicated values of y_t were grouped according to the intervals (less than 0.05), (0.05, 0.09), (0.10, 0.14), ..., (over 0.95), and are presented in table 7.6. There are 123 loans with values of y_t in the interval 0.20 to 0.24, representing 5 percent of all the good and delinquent loans in column 5. In column 6, 11.5 percent of all good and delinquent loans have values of y_t below 0.24.

Table 7.7 presents the relative and cumulative frequency distributions for the values of y_t for the delinquent loans. Column 4 of this table shows that 2.2 percent of the 1,059 delinquent loans have values of y_t in the interval 0.20 to 0.24, and in column 5, 4 percent of the delinquent loans have values of y_t below 0.24.

Using column 6 of table 7.6 and column 5 of table 7.7, it can be seen that 11.5 percent of the good and delinquent loans have values of y_t below 0.24, but only 4 percent of the delinquent loans have y_t values below 0.24. The regression equation thus assigns low y_t values to good loans and high values to delinquent loans, indicating that the equation reported in table 7.5 is a useful tool in discriminating between good and delinquent loans.

From column 6 of table 7.6, the percentage of all loans in the sample having a y_t value below 0.05, below 0.09, etc., was obtained. From column 5 of table

Table 7.5
Coefficients and *F* Ratios of Explanatory Variables in Delinquency Risk

Factor	Coefficient	F Ratio
Loan to Loan Value:		
Over 90%	0.48730*	9.13468
85 – 90%	0.21532	1.67422
Payment to Income:		
Over 30%	0.96224*	16.06260
22 – 30%	0.24256	0.56792
Age of Mortgagor:	−0.01079*	7.70573
Over 50	0.21381*	4.25448
Less than 30	−0.06516	1.10215
Number of Years With Employer	0.00183	0.33521
Age of Property	−0.00317*	5.47683
Unemployment Rate	−0.66183	0.48623
Per Capita Changes in Crimes Against Property	−0.95608	0.14831
Per Capita Changes in Crimes Against Persons	19.20426	0.55920
VA Insurance	0.61604*	75.99899
FHA Insurance	0.07133	1.33797
Price of Property**	−0.00081	1.48555
Number of Children	0.4610*	12.48346
Refinanced Loan	0.28278*	8.78546
Term of Loan	−0.00457	0.61744
Monthly Income**	−0.04422	0.01106
Private Insurance	−0.00002	1.0531
% Change in Population	−0.18848	4.14393

*Statistically significant at the 0.95 level.

**Expressed in dollar amounts. To express in thousands of dollars, move decimal
point three places to the right. Dollar values deflated by the consumer price
index.

Table 7.6
Sample Data: Good Versus Delinquent: Projected Population Data

(1)	(2)	(3)	(4)	(5)	(6)
Values of y_t	Number Good	Number Delinquent	Good and Delinquent	Relative Frequency of Good and Delinquent	Cumulative Frequency of Good and Delinquent
below .05	14	1	15	.006	.006
.05 – .10	20	2	22	.009	.015
.10 – .15	37	4	41	.017	.032
.15 – .20	71	12	83	.034	.065
.20 – .25	100	23	123	.050	.115
.25 – .30	158	47	205	.083	.198
.30 – .35	188	69	257	.104	.303
.35 – .40	169	116	285	.116	.418
.40 – .45	168	105	273	.111	.529
.45 – .50	150	111	261	.106	.635
.50 – .55	122	125	247	.100	.735
.55 – .60	78	101	179	.073	.808
.60 – .65	46	101	147	.060	.868
.65 – .70	42	83	125	.051	.918
.70 – .75	18	53	71	.029	.947
.75 – .80	11	56	67	.027	.974
.80 – .85	7	33	40	.016	.991
.85 – .90	2	5	7	.003	.994
.90 – .95	1	3	4	.002	.995
over .95	3	9	12	.005	1.000

Source: Table 7.5

117

Table 7.7
Sample Data: Good Versus Delinquent: Probability Index

(1)	(2)	(3)	(4)	(5)	(6)
Values of y_t	Number Delinquent	Good and Delinquent	Relative Frequency of Delinquency (Delinquent/ Total Delinquent)	Cumulative Frequency of Delinquency	Probability of Delinquency
less than .05	1	15	.001	.001	.067
.05 – .10	2	22	.002	.003	.091
.10 – .15	4	41	.004	.007	.098
.15 – .20	12	83	.011	.018	.145
.20 – .25	23	123	.022	.040	.187
.25 – .30	47	205	.044	.084	.229
.30 – .35	69	257	.065	.149	.268
.35 – .40	116	285	.110	.259	.407
.40 – .45	105	273	.099	.358	.385
.45 – .50	111	261	.105	.463	.425
.50 – .55	125	247	.118	.581	.506
.55 – .60	101	179	.095	.676	.564
.60 – .65	101	147	.095	.771	.687
.65 – .70	83	125	.078	.849	.664
.70 – .75	53	71	.050	.899	.746
.75 – .80	56	67	.053	.952	.836
.80 – .85	33	40	.031	.983	.825
.85 – .90	5	7	.005	.988	.714
.90 – .95	3	4	.003	.991	.750
over .95	9	12	.009	1.000	.750

Source: Table 7.5.

Figure 7.3
Good Versus Delinquent

% of delinquent loans

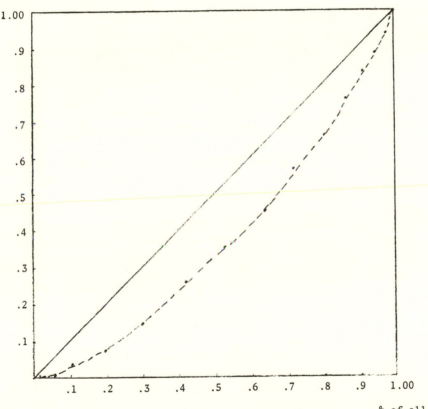

% of all loans

7.7, the percentage of all delinquent loans in the sample having a y_t value below 0.05, below 0.09, etc., was obtained. In figure 7.3, these percentages were plotted against one another and a smooth curve drawn through the points.

As with the good versus foreclosed graph, a regression equation that has low discriminating power will result in a curve near the 45-degree line; the deeper the bow in the curve, the better the discriminating power.

Finally, in column 6 of table 7.7 is presented the value of the ratio of number of delinquent in the interval to number of good and delinquent in the interval for each interval. If the regression equation is a useful discriminator, this ratio should be small for low values of y_t and large for high values. From column 6, we see that the ratio is always below 0.2 for values of y_t below 0.24 and always above 0.5 for values of y_t above 0.54, providing another indication that the pooled good versus delinquent reported in table 7.5 is useful in discriminating between good and delinquent loans.

CHAPTER 8

Evaluating Commercial and Industrial Properties

Lending in the commercial and industrial real estate market can be very attractive and profitable. Commercial banks make a significant part of their mortgage loans in this market, which is rapidly increasing its share of the total mortgage loan portfolios of large- and medium-sized banks. Mortgage-lending activity by savings institutions in the commercial and industrial real estate market has grown significantly and promises to be an increasing proportion of their mortgage portfolios. The pace has quickened following the 1980 and 1982 deregulation of depository institutions. The higher returns offered by industrial and commercial mortgage loans make them rather attractive investment opportunities, but the potential for loss from default and the resulting foreclosure can precipitate serious financial distress for the lending institution when large amounts are involved. It is therefore necessary that an economic, financial, and qualitative analysis be done on each loan application package, to assess both the validity of the assumptions underlying the projections of the cash flows and the risks the lender will assume if the loan is made.

LOAN EVALUATION

In analyzing a loan application, the lender's primary objective is to determine whether the borrower has the capacity to repay the loan punctually as scheduled throughout the life of the loan. The borrower's capacity to repay may depend upon whether the loan is (1) self-liquidating or (2) nonself-liquidating. In a self-liquidating loan, the borrower relies upon the economic benefits, namely, the cash flows generated by the property, to repay the loan. The borrower may or may not have other resources to augment the cash flows from the property. A nonself-liquidating loan is one in which the borrower's capacity to repay is not necessarily tied to the success of the project. The borrower has other resources to meet the mortgage service and may or may not rely on the project cash flows for debt service.

In either case, an economically viable project minimizes the risk exposure of the lender. The viability of the project depends upon the quality of the assumptions and data used in making the projections of revenue, expenditures, and other variables. The lender must ensure that the loan application includes a complete financial analysis and systematically check the validity and robustness of the assumptions, data, and methodology used to generate the forecast of cash flows employed in the analysis.

FINANCIAL ANALYSIS

The mathematics of financial analysis do not incorporate some critical qualitative factors involved in the analysis of real property investment, such as (1) the discontinuities and effects of changes in the environment, (2) the long-term horizon, and (3) the lack of liquidity. Since these factors among others are essential in determining the risks involved in a property, the lender must incorporate their influence in the financial analysis when evaluating the loan package.

The three components of an income-producing real estate investment analysis are

1. *Annual cash flows:* the annual cash inflows from revenues generated, including financing proceeds received, and the cash outflows for operating expenses and mortgage service payments
2. *Tax effects:* the impact of the tax structure on the cash flows from the investment
3. *Capital change:* the effect of reversion of the real estate asset at the end of the holding period on the capital position of the borrower

The analysis that follows is structured to reflect consideration of these components in determining the economic value of the property and the appropriate rate of return over the investment period.

A successful project is one that generates a high net cash flow after taxes with more than adequate coverage of mortgage service and a high return to the investor. Such situations minimize the likelihood of delinquency or default, thus minimizing the lender's risk exposure. From the lender's point of view, the purpose of the loan review is to identify all situations that have the potential of affecting the successful operation of the income-producing capacity of the property during the holding period.

VALUATION

Two kinds of value can be identified in income-producing property: (1) owner value, and (2) market value.

Owner value is based upon special characteristics of a property that an owner finds to be uniquely attractive that may or may not have the same degree of attractiveness to another owner. These comprise pride of ownership and the desire to maintain control of a development or complex, which includes the particular property of interest.

Market value is defined as the most probable price that will result in a transaction between a willing buyer and seller within a reasonable period of time. The market value of a property is influenced by the price trends of comparable properties, the supply and demand pressures, money market conditions, current and expected tax laws, and environmental factors. Three different approaches are used to determine the market value of a property: (1) replacement cost, (2) comparable sales, and (3) income approach. The income approach provides the best measure of value of an income-producing property, and is conceptually superior.

Replacement Cost Approach

The replacement cost approach uses the cost of replacing a property as its value. Replacement cost is associated with the cost of production for duplication or for substitution. Production cost is the sum of land valuation and improvement valuation. The market price of a property is used as the replacement cost if the property can easily be substituted in the market, and it is lower than the cost of duplicating the property. Otherwise, the duplication cost is used as the replacement cost when it is lower than the substitution cost.

Comparable Sales or Market Approach

Risk Class and Comparable Value

It is held that all assets compete for the investor's dollar; more specifically, all assets in the same risk class must be of comparable value to the investor. If not, the investor would profit through arbitrage by moving from a higher-priced to a lower-priced asset. In an efficient market where all information is available to every investor, assets in the same risk class will carry comparable market value.

This concept of risk class forms the basis for the use of comparable market value as a method for valuation. This approach indicates that the market value of other properties that are very closely comparable with the property being valued can be used as surrogates for its value.

Finding comparable properties may or may not be an easy task. It may not be difficult finding comparable properties for general purpose commercial buildings, for example, office buildings, warehouses, shopping centers, and shopping malls. There are three important factors that affect property costs that must be considered in determining comparability: (1) location; (2) construction, size, design; and (3) use.

Location is a very important factor in real estate. Two buildings of the same construction and use, but not in the same or a comparable location, can have substantially different values owing to differences in the market demand for the buildings. For example, identical buildings, one situated in a city and the other in a rural area, would carry significantly different values. This is very common among residential properties. Real estate tends to be location specific; it is therefore important that the location of properties used as comparables be within the same or similar real estate market area.

Construction is another important factor in determining comparability, since construction cost can be very different for two properties if they are structurally dissimilar and the materials used are very different. In addition, the age of the building may have some impact on the cost of construction and the book value, because an older building with much shorter remaining potential economic life would have a much lower economic value than a building of more recent vintage with relatively longer potential economic life.

The use to which a building can be put is the third important factor in comparability. General purpose buildings like offices can be easily compared with other office buildings in the same vicinity, with adjustments for vintage and construction costs. Special purpose buildings are more difficult to deal with, since they are built for specific uses.

The Gross Income Multiplier

The market approach uses the gross income multiplier concept in determining the market value:

$$\text{gross income multiplier} = \frac{\text{price}}{\text{gross annual income}}.$$

The gross income multiplier is the multiple of the annual income in the price of the property. It is obtained by dividing the price by the gross annual income. Conceptually, it is presumed that the price is a multiple of the periodic annual income through which the investor recoups the investment in the property plus a return on the investment. The multiple that the market uses for an investment property is based upon (1) the size of the annual cash flows, (2) the payback period for properties of that risk class, (3) the inherent investment value of that type of property, and (4) its location. An average of the gross income multipliers of comparable properties is used to embody the element of comparability. The gross income multiplier is a generalized measure computed by taking the average multiple of comparable properties.

To find the market value of property Y, the comparable value approach is used. The prices and gross income of properties A, B, C, D, and E that are assumed comparable are used to compute the gross income multiplier, which is then used to calculate the market value of property Y.

Example 8.1. Computation of the market (comparable) value of a property:

	Comparable Properties (000's)				
	A	B	C	D	E
Price	1,500	1,500	1,300	1,600	2,000
Gross income	180	250	150	210	280
Gross multiplier: price/income	8.33	7.20	8.67	7.62	7.14

Gross multiplier average = 7.79

Next, the gross multiplier average is used to compute the market value of property Y with gross income of $190,000 by multiplying the gross income by the average gross multiplier:

Gross income	$ 190,000
Average gross income multiplier	× 7.79 .
Market value of property	$1,480,000

This property is considered comparable with the five properties A to E, because, among other factors of comparability, its gross income of $190,000 falls within the range of gross incomes of the five properties from $150,000 to $280,000. The market value obtained is the benchmark price, which is adjusted to reflect special characteristics of property Y and its investment appeal relative to the other properties.

The gross income multiplier, as its name implies, is simply a multiplication factor conceptually similar to the common stock price/earning ratio, which is used to multiply its earnings per share to obtain the price of the stock. The reciprocal of the gross income multiplier is the gross return for the income period. It is important to note that the gross income multiplier itself is not a return and cannot be interpreted as such.

Income Approach

In the income approach, the value of an asset is determined through the interplay of the forces of demand and supply. An asset competes with every other asset in the same risk class for the investor's dollar, and the attractiveness of the asset as an investment vehicle is based upon how much cash it returns to the investor for each dollar of investment. Given its risk class, the asset with the highest return is most attractive and logically has the highest value to the investor. Similarly, of all properties with the same return, the one with the lowest risk has the highest value to the investor.

Return on Investment

Return is measured by the proportional relationship of the income produced by the asset over what was paid for it. The concept of return expressed as a proportion of the investment value is a simplified measure of return used for expository purposes. Alternative concepts of return will be discussed later in the chapter. This relationship is formulated as follows:

$$\text{return} = \frac{\text{cash stream}}{\text{amount invested}} = \frac{C}{I}. \tag{8.1}$$

To illustrate the concept of return on investment in relation to asset value, two examples are presented, showing the returns from two assets sold at the same price initially with two different levels of cash flows to the investor.

Example 8.2. Asset A priced at $1,000 produces a cash stream of $100 a year. Its return is

$$\text{return (A)} = \frac{\$100}{\$1,000} = 0.10, \text{ or 10 percent.}$$

Asset A produces a 10 percent return.

Example 8.3. Asset B priced at $1,000 produces a cash stream of $110 a year.

$$\text{return (B)} = \frac{\$110}{\$1,000} = 0.11, \text{ or 11 percent.}$$

A comparison of the two returns in examples 8.2 and 8.3 shows that asset B's return of 11 percent (equivalently expressed as 11 cents in the dollar), is higher than asset A's return of 10 percent, or 10 cents on the dollar. In other words, asset B returns 11 cents as compared with 10 cents returned by asset A for every dollar invested. Asset B demonstrably is worth more than asset A, even though the prices of the two assets are the same. Investors would value asset B more than asset A, because asset B generates a greater cash return than asset A. In general, a property is worth more in investment value if it produces a greater cash return per dollar of investment than other properties in the same risk class (comparable properties).

Generalized Valuation Formula

From the relationship expressed in equation (8.1), the investment required to produce a cash flow equivalent to a given percentage return can easily be derived. Using example 8.3, to find the investment that would produce a $110 cash return, it is necessary to find out how many 11 cents are in $110. This can be stated as follows:

$110 is to I_B as 11 cents is to $1.

$$\frac{I_B}{\$1} = \frac{\$110}{\$0.11}; \text{ then } I_B = \frac{\$110}{0.11} = \$1,000.$$

In general,

$$\text{investment} = \frac{\text{cash stream}}{\text{rate of return}}, \tag{8.2}$$

which is expressed in compact notation as

$$I_B = \frac{c}{r}. \qquad (8.3)$$

Equation (8.2) is referred to as the generalized valuation formula used to find the value of an investment asset. The capitalization of the cash stream, the rate of return (r), is called the "capitalization rate," and I_B is the computed value of the asset.

Net Present Value Approach to Valuation

In the net present value approach, the future net cash flows generated by the property during each period of the investment and the net cash flow from reversion are discounted by an appropriate rate of return to obtain their present worth. The sum of the present worth of the cash inflows less the present worth of the initial investment gives the net present value, which is the computed market value of the property.

The cash stream and the capitalization rate are the two key components of valuation. It is therefore necessary to examine each of these components to gain full understanding of their makeup and role in valuation. There is continuing controversy in the literature over the relevant cash flows and capitalization rate. Several of the areas of controversy will be explored to gain some understanding of the nature of the dispute. It is useful for lending officers and institutions involved in mortgage lending to become familiar with the different perspectives to enable them to utilize these insights in their analysis and decision making.

The Cash Stream

The Cash stream of a property is made up of the cash inflows and outflows. The "setup" is a financial accounting statement used to measure the cash stream from which the net cash flow of a property is obtained. The structure of the setup is discussed below.

The Setup

In the field of real estate, a setup is a hybrid combination of an income statement and a cash flow statement. It is designed to produce a better measure of value of real property than either of the two statements can produce alone. The setup shows the amount of carrying cost over time and the amount of money at risk in holding the property, from which a measure of the opportunity cost of investing in the property can be obtained. Table 8.1 presents an outline of a setup statement from which the pretax cash flow and the tax effects are derived. The elements of the setup are discussed in the following sections to give detailed insights into their relative significance.

Table 8.1
Setup Statement for Income-Producing Properties

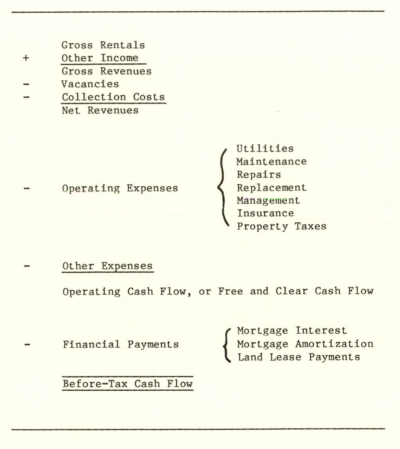

Elements of the Setup

In this section, each element of the setup is discussed, followed by an examination of how changes within the element are caused by different properties. The different types of properties covered in the discussion are office buildings, commercial and industrial space, commercial apartment complexes, and raw land.

Gross Revenues. The primary cash inflow of income-producing properties is from rental income, which together with cash from other income sources make up the gross revenues. Since rental income makes up the bulk of gross revenues, the rental structure is very important in the determination of the size of the gross revenues. The rent structure must be competitive in order to attract tenants. It is necessary to obtain information on ''comparable'' rents of similar properties.

Baseline Data. The first step in the collection of local market data is the gathering of baseline data on comparables from primary survey sources such as the local chamber of commerce, the state, county, or city agencies, the local newspapers, and the metropolitan area real estate board. Information on office, commercial, and industrial space may not always be available at the local level, especially if the property is for specialized use. Other sources of information include specialized journals such as regional real estate reviews; listings of office, industrial, and commercial space by major real estate brokers; and local sources from other major metropolitan areas around the country.

The rents and prices obtained from other real estate markets reflect the demand and supply forces operating in those markets that may or may not be operating in the local market. These forces include market strength, financial strength of the prospective tenants, whether or not the tenant assumes financial responsibility to make improvements, etc. The rental information obtained from other real estate market sources should be used as reference prices only in determining the rental structure in the local market. Negotiations of the terms of each lease will determine the exact rent. It is important to collect as much useful data as possible, and analyze those collected, to get all the information available in the data set. Characteristics that make properties comparable include such internal features as layout, decor, adequacy of utilities, and maintenance facilities and exterior features such as views, access to transportation, etc.

Competition. The next task is to determine to what extent the property can compete given its location, architectural style, construction, interior and exterior features, etc. A careful assessment of how effectively the property can compete is necessary, since an incorrect assessment could result in either a rent structure that is too high, which would cause a higher vacancy rate to occur, or one that is too low, with the attendant loss of revenue.

Trend. Commercial and industrial leases are generally long term in duration. The short-term effects of changes in government policy and inflationary trends may not have much impact on these leases, except when they are due for renewal. Leases of shorter duration provide opportunity to adjust rents upward when price levels are rising. It is therefore important to study and project trends before the rent structure is set.

Vacancies. Once the rental structure has been set up, the vacancy rate determines the size of the gross revenue. It tells the number of units that are not rented and are therefore not producing revenue at any given period of time. The higher the vacancy rate, the larger is the number of units not rented and the lower the gross revenue. Because of its impact upon the gross revenue, the vacancy rate is very important; it is the second element shown in the setup. When this rate is not taken into account in the setup, this has the effect of inflating the gross revenue above its real level; the property then generally appears more profitable than it really is, and therefore more attractive as an investment. This increases the riskiness of the property, since the potential gross revenue is actually lower, reflecting the vacancies not included.

Comparable data for vacancies are generally more difficult to assess for office, commercial, and industrial properties. Information on gross area vacancies are available for the standard metropolitan statistical areas. The board of realtors and other civic agencies have data on office vacancy rates in larger cities. Information may be obtained from reviews on the changing market scene in the *National Real Estate Investor,* and annually updated historical data for most real estate markets are provided by the *Real Estate Analyst.*

Because of its direct impact on the gross revenues, it is necessary for lenders to become familiar with trends in the vacancy rate, as well as prospective new entries into the real estate market that might have adverse effects on the property being evaluated. In assessing the overall trends in vacancy rates, such forces as growth in service industries, consumer spending patterns, and national economic trends should be taken into consideration. In the local market, the number of building permits issued, or the number of applications for building permits, is a good indication of new entries that would increase the supply of office, commercial, or industrial space. Matching the present and future supply to the total potential demand would indicate the vacancy rates that might prevail in the future.

Landlords are usually apt to create special attractive deals for their tenants in order to increase occupancy rates and reduce vacancy rates. Many of the special deals are not without costs, and have the effect of reducing the gross revenues or increasing the operating costs. Lenders must be aware of when a property being evaluated has been subjected to occupancy boosters that may affect the future vacancy rates.

For apartment buildings, the rental boards publish vacancy rates, and the FHA compiles statistics reported in the *Real Estate Analyst.* The Census Bureau publishes numbers and rates of vacancies every five years. For analysis of new developments, the lender must be cognizant of the leasing terms in the locality, current practices on concessions, and the extent to which management absorbs the costs.

Other Income. "Other income," as the term implies, is income from sources other than rent. For commercial and industrial properties, other income sources are parking, janitorial services, security, etc. The other income category is usually stable once established, except for the effect of changes in the vacancy rate. A lender should examine the agreements or the leases underlying these charges, and the assumptions underlying projections of other income, to be sure of the reliability of these sources.

Sources of other income for apartment complexes include utility fees, recreational club membership, laundry fees and rentals, parking charges, and furniture rental. These facilities are usually very profitable and add to the attractiveness of the investment. It is important that the basis for income forecast be closely scrutinized to determine that the sources are in accordance with local practices for charges on the services.

Operating Expenses. Operating expenses include all items of expenditure and payments before mortgage debt servicing and lease charges. As indicated in table 8.1, operating expenses are deducted from net revenues to obtain the operating cash flow, otherwise called the "free and clear" cash flow. The operating cash flow available for mortgage debt servicing declines as operating expenses rise, which can impair the borrower's ability to carry out mortgage debt service, thereby increasing the risk of delinquency and default. Furthermore, a decline in the free and clear cash flow may result in a lower before-tax cash flow and decreased profitability. The control of operating expenses is a key element in assessing real estate profitability. It is important in analyzing the setup for the loan officer to appraise the validity of the information presented on operating expenses and the reliability of the assumptions underlying the projections used as a basis for future expenses. The best available information should be obtained for estimating the operating expenses since unreliable, incomplete information or discontinuities in the data set may result in significant upward biases in various items of the operating expense that could impair the future mortgage-servicing ability of the mortgagor. It is important to verify that all relevant items of operating expenses are included, since the omission of any item may distort the potential liquidity and profitability of the property. Sellers might, on occasion, leave out an item or two of operating expense to make the property look more profitable and attractive to potential buyers.

The following conceptual framework is useful in developing and analyzing operating expenses. There are three primary types of expenses that vary (1) in relation to the gross rent; (2) with the space involved, in square feet or cubic feet; and (3) with the number of units. The differences in the types of expenses must be taken into account when forecasts of future profitability are being developed or evaluated.

The following categories of expenses will be analyzed: maintenance, repairs, replacement, insurance, utilities, property taxes, advertising, management, and rental. There are subcategories within each that should be considered in each case. Conceptually, analysis of the subcategories follows that of the category of which they are a part.

Maintenance. The nature of maintenance expense is somewhat complex because there are a number of factors that affect its level and cost. The factors that affect maintenance cost include age, design, type of construction and materials used, number and sizes of public spaces, quality of original equipment installed, type of heating and air conditioning, type of and material used in flooring, accessibility of windows, etc. These factors have a differential impact on the level and cost of maintenance.

Generally, more maintenance is required on older buildings, as structural components and equipment wear down, than on newly constructed buildings. The design, type of construction, and materials used in the construction, to some degree, are key determinants of the level of maintenance required. Usually, there is also more maintenance done in public spaces within and around the building. Equipment such as elevators, escalators, heating and cooling units, etc., normally require maintenance. The condition and age of the equipment, in addition to their life histories, must be taken into account in determining the level of maintenance involved. The care of floors in a building is very important. Greater care is required for some types of flooring materials and construction. Similarly, the accessibility of windows determines the cost of their maintenance, especially if scaffolding is required to reach them.

Firms that provide maintenance services for various types of building equipment, floors, and windows have contract prices that can be used as a basis for assessing the cost of upkeep. These prices do include significant profit margins that should be taken into account.

Repairs. Repairs relate to major repairs to building, plant, and equipment, since minor repairs are routinely carried out during maintenance. Repairs involve fixing malfunctioning equipment and broken items as well as replacement of component parts. Heating and cooling equipment need periodic repairs, as do broken windows and doors and leaking faucets. Older equipment generally requires more extensive repairs at higher costs.

As the equipment gets older in apartment buildings, disposals, dishwashers, refrigerators, and stoves require systematic scheduling of repairs to keep the tenants contented and satisfied.

Adequate provision should be made for the cost of all anticipated and unanticipated repairs in the operating expenses of the setup. When the cost of repairs is not properly budgeted, the actual cost may at times vary significantly from the budget, and this may result in higher operating costs and lower operating cash flow.

Reserve for Replacement. Buildings and equipment suffer wear and tear through normal use that limit their economic life, after which they have to be replaced. Replacement reserves are periodic charges against revenue to provide cash set aside for the replacement of the items as needed. Without reserves for replacement, new expenditure is required for replacement of items financed from equity or a loan or bought on credit. If the replacement is financed through a loan, a higher debt service results, increasing the debt service burden on the operating cash flow. Financing on credit may require a short repayment period, resulting in a heavy drain on cash. Each of these financing methods impacts on liquidity and the ability to service the mortgage debt.

In the absence of replacement reserves, it is important to recognize the impact of replacement expenditure on the cash flow from an investment. In cases where the seller has neglected repairs and replacement in anticipation of a sale to pass on the burden, replacement may be required in existing properties much earlier than anticipated. Technical appraisal may not uncover all problem situations that can arise after the transfer has been finalized. Unlike depreciation, replacement reserves generally are not tax deductible; but the cost of items like painting or component parts may be expensed, since these expenses represent the cash equivalents of depreciation charges previously taken.

In the case of commercial and industrial leases, the primary responsibility for replacement is usually that of the tenant.

Insurance. Insurance on an existing property is usually verifiable. It should be adequate to cover the replacement cost of the structure or building at current prices. Two situations arising in many insurance policies may affect the insured: (1) insufficient coverage to meet replacement cost and (2) too much insurance for the coverage needed. The first case of inadequate coverage puts both the lender and the mortgagor at risk. In case of fire or other disaster, the insurance proceeds would not be sufficient to replace the structure. The lender's loss would be limited to the difference between the insurance proceeds available for payoff and the mortgage balance outstanding. If the mortgage balance is greater than the amount of insurance coverage, the lender could lose the excess of the mortgage balance above the insurance proceeds available for payoff. In the second case, the amount of insurance covers the mortgage balance outstanding, which includes both the land value and the cost of the structure and improvements. No insurance coverage is needed for the land since it is not destructible by fire. In areas where land values are high, as in the case of downtown commercial sites, the cost of land could be a substantial part of the mortgage balance. For example, if the land value is 25 percent of the mortgage balance, and if the insurance premium is $1 million, the overpayment amounts to $250,000 a year. This amount could be saved through reduction of the operating expense, which increases the operating cash flow available to meet mortgage service charges.

The lender enjoys greater safety in the second case when the insurance covers the mortgage balance, but this can contribute to illiquidity and probable delinquency or default, which are presumed to be of greater risk to the lender. Since land values do not normally depreciate, except in declining neighborhoods, it may appear in the interest of both the lender and the investor to limit insurance coverage to the replacement cost of buildings, structures, and improvements destructible by fire.

Utilities. The cost of utilities for heating and cooling fluctuates with the cost of the fuels used by the power-generating companies. Since the early 1970s, the cost of utilities has risen significantly. Until the higher cost can be passed on to the tenants in higher rents, rising costs increase operating expenses and decrease operating cash flows. Higher utility cost can be passed on to tenants more easily in short-term than in long-term leases. When utilities are the responsibility of the landlord, provision should be made for pass-through of rising utility cost in long-term leases.

Real Estate Taxes. Real estate taxes generally increase from year to year to meet the revenue needs of the local municipality or county. Four factors that are precursors to increases in real estate tax rates are (1) population increase, (2) expansion of municipal services, (3) new schools, and (4) major public facilities and projects.

Changes in valuation assessments are carried out periodically to reflect increasing real estate values, and the higher property assessments cause real estate taxes to increase. When a property is sold, the higher new market price forms the basis for new valuation assessment, resulting in significant increases in real estate taxes. Provision should be made for the potentially higher taxes when the purchaser is paying much more than the assessed valuation for the property. It is useful to examine the assessed valuation of comparable properties and their taxes when purchasing in the locality. The strength of tax escalation clauses in leases should also be considered.

The lender should be cognizant of the impact of real estate taxes on the profitability and liquidity of a real estate investment and how they affect the mortgagor's ability to carry out the mortgage servicing.

Advertising. The amount of advertising done is directly correlated with vacancy rates and the amount of competition in the area. Advertising is usually accomplished through newspapers, magazines, and billboards. The fees for billboards are standard, but can be negotiated. In general, advertising expense is a relatively minor, and controllable, item in the operating expenses. It may rise significantly when vacancy rates increase.

Rental and Management. Professional property management companies are usually hired to manage larger commercial, industrial, and apartment complexes. Management expense could be significant and should be included in the setup since its omission could seriously distort the operating profit and reduce the profitability and liquidity available for debt service. Rental expenses may be combined with the management fee when the property is under the control of a professional manager.

Other Expenses. Other expenses are of extraordinary nature but specifically related to the property under consideration, such as security expenses, fire protection, etc. In commercial and industrial properties, these items should normally be small amounts. In apartment buildings, these expenditures could be substantial and should be reflected in the rent.

FINANCIAL ANALYSIS

An example of financial analysis of property investment is presented to illustrate the process of developing a complete assessment of the financial feasibility of two commercial properties for which loan applications have been made and which are being evaluated by the lender for loan approval. Two properties are used to show (1) comparable analysis and (2) treatment of leasehold versus outright purchase of land.

Case 8.1: Northridge office park condominiums. A loan application for a first mortgage on the Northridge office park condominiums located in a suburban location of a major metropolitan area, in an attractive community with a lot of commercial and residential developments. The mortgage request is for $4,500,000.

Case 8.2: Vining office complex. A loan application for a first mortgage on the Vining office complex located about 10 miles to the west of the Northridge office condominium park. The Vining office complex is located in a fast-growing county, with a proliferation of office parks and residential developments. The mortgage request is for $4,900,000.

Detailed information on the two properties is presented in table 8.2.
The Northridge and Vining properties are comparable in many respects, al-

Table 8.2
Financial Data for Northridge and Vining Properties

	Northridge	Vining
No. of Units	100	105
Gross Purchase Price	$4,800,000	$5,300,000
Equity Investment	$300,000	$400,000
Amount of 1st Mortgage	$4,500,000	$4,900,000
Interest Rate	8%	8.5%
Term	30 year	20 years
Amortization Period	30 years	40 years
Constant	8.883%	8.386%
Net Operating Income	$480,000	$490,000
Leasehold Payments	$50,000	--
Depreciable Base	$4,800,000	$5,150,000
Economic Life	40 years	40 years
Method of Depreciation	200% Decl.	200% Decl.
Estimated Sale Price	$5,200,000	$6,100,000
Expected Year of Sale	8	8

Table 8.3
Project Setups (000's)

		Northridge	Vining	
Gross Rents		840.00	825.00	
– Vacancies	(5%)	42.00	25.00	(3%)
Net Rents		798.00	800.00	
– Operating Expenses		217.20	211.00	
– Real Estate Taxes		100.80	99.00	
Net Operating Income (Free and Clear)		480.00	490.00	
– Finance Payments		399.74	410.91	
– Lease Payments		50.00	--	
Before Tax Cash Flow		30.26	79.09	

though the purchase price of Vining is $500,000 higher than that of Northridge. Both properties are located in the same general area, with locations similar in attractiveness and land values.

Project Setup

The setups for the two office projects are presented in table 8.3. Annual gross rents for Northridge of $840,000 are slightly higher than those for Vining of $825,000. The vacancy rate of 5 percent for Northridge is higher than the 3 percent at Vining. The land at Northridge is leased, while the land at Vining is owned outright. The setup shows a before-tax cash flow of $30,260 for Northridge as compared with $79,090 for Vining. Three factors account for Northridge's lower before-tax cash flow: (1) higher expected vacancy rate, (2) higher operating expenses, and (3) leasehold payments of $50,000 a year.

Since the project setup is a pro forma analysis, it is useful to examine the effect of assumptions made on two key factors: (1) vacancies and (2) operating expenses. A low vacancy rate assumption is more attractive than a high rate because it makes the before-tax cash flow higher. If the actual vacancy rate and the actual operating expenses are higher than in the forecast, the actual net operating income will also be lower. Significant differences between the projections in the setup and the actual results could impair the ability of the mortgagor to meet mortgage finance payments to the lender, thereby increasing the lender's risk exposure.

In table 8.3, the higher before-tax cash flow makes the Vining project more attractive than the Northridge project.

RATIO ANALYSIS: OPERATING COMPARABLES

The relative, and absolute, attractiveness of the projects can be gleaned from a ratio analysis of the operating comparables, presented in table 8.4. Elements of the setup in table 8.3 are used to compute the ratios in this table. A discussion of them is presented below.

Operating Ratios

1. *Annual operating expenses per unit* shows that it costs $162, or 8.6 percent, more to operate a unit at Northridge than at Vining. The lower operating unit expense compensates for the higher purchase cost at Vining. The objective is to keep the operating expense per unit to the minimum acceptable level, as the operating expense has a direct impact on the operating income, or "free cash flow."

2. *Operating expense as a percentage of gross revenue* indicates what proportion of gross revenue is operating expense. Both projects are roughly the same in this regard. It is usually possible to obtain local, regional, and national statistics on operating expense per unit and operating expense as a ratio of gross revenue, from which comparison can be made with the projects under review. Again, the importance of keeping operating expenses in line cannot be overstated.

3. *Real estate taxes as a percentage of gross revenue* is the same for both projects at 12 percent. It so happens in this case that the two projects are located in contiguous counties, with essentially the same tax rates. This is not always the case. Real estate tax is the product of assessed valuation and the millage tax rate, either of which can be raised by the taxing authority to meet revenue needs. The tax rate assumed in the setup must therefore reflect future revenue needs of the local government.

Profitability Ratios

4. *Return on equity* is computed by dividing the average annual net cash flow by equity, which gives the net cash flow per dollar of equity invested. Vining's return on equity of 19.78 percent is almost twice the 10.09 percent for Northridge.

5. *Total return on equity excluding reversion* is obtained by dividing the average annual total cash return before reversion by the equity. Northridge's 31.08 percent is higher than Vining's 29.03 percent. Since Vining has a substantially higher return on equity, Northridge's higher total return before reversion derives from the greater tax savings that result from its lower rental income and payment of leasehold rent.

Table 8.4
Financial Ratio Analyses

Ratio	Formula For Calculation	Calculations Northridge	Calculations Vining
Operating			
1. Annual Operating Expenses Per Unit	Annual Operating Expenses / No. of Units	$\dfrac{\$217,200}{100} = \$2,172$	$\dfrac{\$211,000}{\$105} = \$2,010$
2. Operating Expense as Percentage of Gross Revenue	Operating Expenses / Gross Revenue	$\dfrac{\$217}{\$840} = 25.83\%$	$\dfrac{\$211}{\$825} = 25.58\%$
3. Real Estate Taxes as Percentage of Gross Revenue	Real Estate Taxes / Gross Revenue	$\dfrac{\$100.80}{\$840} = 12\%$	$\dfrac{\$99}{\$825} = 12\%$
Profitability			
4. Return on Equity	Average Annual Net Cash Flow / Equity	$\dfrac{\$30.26}{\$300} = 10.09\%$	$\dfrac{\$79.09}{\$400} = 19.78\%$
5. Total Return on Equity: Excluding Reversion	Average Annual Total Cash Returned / Equity	$\dfrac{\$93.23}{\$300} = 31.08\%$	$\dfrac{\$116.10}{\$400} = 29.03\%$
6. Total Return on Equity	Cumulative Total Cash Returned / Equity	$\dfrac{\$863.26}{\$300} = 2.88 \text{ times}$	$\dfrac{\$1406.19}{\$400} = 3.52 \text{ times}$
Leverage			
7. Debt Service Coverage	Net Operating Income / Debt Service	$\dfrac{\$480}{\$399.74} = 1.2 \text{ times}$	$\dfrac{\$490}{\$410.91} = 1.19 \text{ times}$
8. Fixed Charges Coverage	Net Operating Income / Debt Service plus Lease Rent	$\dfrac{\$480}{\$449.74} = 1.06 \text{ times}$	$\dfrac{\$490}{\$410.91} = 1.19 \text{ times}$

6. *Total return on equity* is computed by dividing the cumulative total cash return, including the net cash flows from reversion, by the equity. The gain from sale at reversion usually increases the total cash flow significantly, making the total return on equity a multiple of the equity invested. Vining's total return on equity of 3.52 is much higher than Northridge's return of 2.88.

Leverage Ratios

7. *Debt service coverage* is determined by dividing the net operating income (free cash flow) by the debt service. The ratio measures the extent to which the net operating income can decline before the firm is unable to meet its debt service. Failure to meet the debt service can result in delinquency, legal action by the lender, and foreclosure. This ratio is therefore of particular importance to lenders when reviewing the setup and in assessing the potential riskiness of the project. Debt service coverages for the two projects are approximately the same.

8. *Fixed charges coverage* measures the extent to which the net operating income (or free cash flow) covers the fixed charges that must be met regularly and punctually to avoid legal measures or foreclosure action. The fixed charges paid from the net operating income are the debt service and the lease payments. To obtain the fixed charges coverage ratio, the net operating income in table 8.3 is divided by the debt service plus lease rents paid. Northridge's fixed charges coverage is only 1.06 times, a rather thin coverage of the fixed charges. If vacancy rates or operating expenses rise, Northridge's operating income may not cover its fixed charges, which may lead the lender or leaseholder to institute legal action. The lease payments for the land at Northridge increase its fixed charges. Since Vining does not have any lease payments, the fixed charges coverage ratio is the same as the debt service ratio. This highlights one aspect of the difference in treatments of leasehold as opposed to freehold, or outright, ownership.

RISK AND BREAK-EVEN OCCUPANCY POINT

The occupancy rate is the key determinant of the amount of gross revenue, and must therefore be watched very closely. It is vitally important for control purposes to know the level of occupancy at which the project would break even and the amount of margin that is available to work with.

Table 8.5 presents a break-even analysis of the occupancy rate projected for each of the two properties. The break-even occupancy can be expressed in terms of the number of units, or the percentage of units, at which total revenue equals total cost. Given the projected vacancy rate, net rent is the total revenue expected. The total cost includes all operating expenses, real estate taxes, finance payments, and lease payments. At the break-even point, where net rent equals all expenses and payments, the before-tax cash flow will be zero. The break-even vacancy point can then be expressed in terms of the total cash outflow before tax as a percentage of gross rents:

$$\text{break-even point} = \frac{\text{vacancy} + \text{operating expenses} + \text{debt service}}{\text{gross rents}}$$

$$= \frac{217.20 + 100.80 + 399.74 + 50.00}{840.00} \times 100 = 91.39 \text{ percent.}$$

The break-even point can also be obtained in terms of net cash inflow excluding the before-tax cash flow as a percentage of gross rents:

$$\text{break-even point} = \frac{\text{net rents} - \text{before-tax cash flow}}{\text{gross rents}} \times 100$$

$$= \frac{798.00 - 30.26}{840.00} = 91.39 \text{ percent.}$$

This indicates that the occupancy rate of Northridge could fall to 91.39 percent, a vacancy rate of 8.61 percent, and enough cash from net rents would still be available to cover all costs in the setup, providing an additional 3.61 percent vacancy margin beyond the projected vacancy rate of 5 percent.

The break-even point for Vining, as shown in table 8.5, is 87.38 percent, providing an additional vacancy margin of 9.62 percent beyond the projected vacancy rate of 3 percent. In the Vining project, occupancy rates could fall to 87.38 percent and the project could still cover all the expense payments and the real estate taxes in the setup.

The break-even point for Vining is 4.4 percentage points higher than the break-even point for Northridge, which indicates that Vining has more flexibility in covering expenses and financial payments than Northridge, which translates to relatively lower risk for the Vining property.

AFTER-TAX CASH FLOW

Tables 8.6a and 8.6b present the computation of the projected net cash return after reversion for the seven years that the Northridge and Vining properties would be operated before reversion.

Table 8.5
Break-Even Analysis of Occupancy Rate

	Northridge	Vining
Occupancy: Current and Projected	95.00%	97.00%
Break-even Occupancy	91.39%	87.38%
Vacancy Margin	3.61%	9.62%

Table 8.6a
Projected Annual Net Cash Return After Reversion: Northridge (000's)

	1987	1988	1989	1990	1991	1992	1993
Net Operating Income Before Debt Service	480.00	480.00	480.00	480.00	480.00	480.00	480.00
- Leasehold Payment	50.00	50.00	50.00	50.00	50.00	50.00	50.00
- Mortgage Interest	399.74	399.74	399.74	399.74	399.74	399.74	399.74
Before-Tax Cash Flow	30.26	30.26	30.26	30.26	30.26	30.26	30.26
+ Amortization	39.75	42.93	46.36	50.07	54.08	58.40	63.07
- Depreciation	240.00	228.00	216.60	205.77	195.48	185.71	176.42
Net Taxable Income	(169.99)	(154.81)	(139.98)	(125.44)	(111.14)	(97.05)	(83.05)
Tax Savings @ 50% tax rate	85.00	77.41	69.99	62.72	55.57	48.53	41.55
+ (Add back) Before Tax Cash Flow	30.26	30.26	30.26	30.26	30.26	30.26	30.26
Annual Cash Return Before Reversion	115.26	107.67	100.25	92.98	85.83	78.79	71.81
+ Reversion of Net Cash from Sale	--	--	--	--	--	--	210.67
Total Cash Return After Reversion	115.26	107.67	100.25	92.98	85.83	78.79	282.48
Cumulative Cash Return	115.26	222.93	323.18	416.16	501.99	580.78	863.26

Table 8.6b
Projected Annual Net Cash Return After Reversion: Vining (000's)

	1987	1988	1989	1990	1991	1992	1993
Net Operating Income before Debt Service	490.00	490.00	490.00	490.00	490.00	490.00	490.00
- Leasehold Payment	--	--	--	--	--	--	--
- Mortgage Interest	410.91	410.91	410.91	410.91	410.91	410.91	410.91
Before-Tax Cash Flow	79.09	79.09	79.09	79.09	79.09	79.09	79.09
+ Amortization	54.00	58.32	62.99	68.02	73.47	79.34	85.69
- Depreciation	257.50	249.63	232.39	220.77	209.74	199.25	189.29
Net Taxable Income	(124.41)	(114.34)	(90.31)	(73.66)	(57.18)	(40.82)	(24.51)
- Tax Savings @ 50% tax rate	62.21	53.61	45.16	36.83	28.59	20.41	12.26
+ Before-Tax Cash Flow (added back)	79.09	79.09	79.09	79.09	79.09	79.09	79.09
Annual Cash Return Before Reversion	141.30	132.70	124.25	115.92	107.68	99.50	91.36
+ Reversion of Net Cash from sale	--	--	--	--	--	--	593.48
Total Cash Return After Reversion	141.30	132.70	124.25	115.92	107.68	99.50	684.84
Cumulative Cash Return	141.30	274.00	398.25	514.17	621.85	721.35	1,406.19

To present a complete picture of the financial cash inflows and outflows, the free and clear cash flow is reproduced from table 8.3. The recapture by the mortgagor of the amortization of the equity investment is added to the before-tax cash flow, and the depreciation charge is deducted to obtain the taxable income. The effect of accelerated depreciation on the cash flow is incorporated by using a 200 percent double-declining balance as the basis for the depreciation schedule. The accelerated depreciation charge-off results in a negative taxable income, or a loss produces a tax saving equal to 50 percent of the negative taxable income. Using the current 50 percent marginal tax rate, the loss in the after-tax cash flow for each year is added to the before-tax cash flow to obtain the annual cash return before reversion.[1] This is the cash flow that will accrue to the mortgagor during the years the project is operated before reversion.

NET CASH FROM SALE

At the end of the seventh year, the two properties are sold. To arrive at the net cash flow to the mortgagor from the sale, the excess depreciation above the straight line must be recaptured from the gain from sale, before the capital gain is derived, and the capital gains tax computed to arrive at the closing income tax liability. The gain from sale on reversion is shown in table 8.7. The computation of the excess depreciation recapture on reversion is presented in table 8.8, and the closing income tax liability on reversion shown in table 8.9 is the sum of the tax on the capital gain from the sale and the excess depreciation recapture. In table 8.10, the net cash from sale on reversion is derived by deducting the final income tax liability and the outstanding mortgage balance from the sale price. This is the final cash inflow to the mortgagor.

The net cash flow from sale is then included with the after tax cash flows in tables 8.6a and 8.6b to obtain the total net cash inflows to the mortgagor.

Table 8.7
Gain From Sale on Reversion

	Northridge	Vining
Sales Price	5,200,000	6,100,000
– Net Book Value	3,352,020	3,596,430
Gain on Sale	1,847,980	2,503,570

Table 8.8
Excess Depreciation Recapture on Reversion

	Northridge	Vining
Accumulated Depreciation	1,447,980	1,553,570
- Straight Line Depreciation	840,000	901,250
Excess Depreciation	607,980	652,320
Tax Rate	0.50	0.50
Excess Depreciation Recapture	303,990	326,160

Table 8.9
Income Tax Liability on Reversion

	Northridge	Vining
Gain From Sale	1,847,980	2,503,570
- Excess Depreciation	303,990	326,160
Capital Gain	1,543,990	2,177,410
Capital Gain Tax	0.35	0.35
Capital Gain Tax	540,397	762,094
+ Excess Depreciation Recapture	303,990	326,160
Income Tax Liability	844,387	1,088,254

Table 8.10
Net Cash from Sale on Reversion

	Northridge	Vining
Sale Price	5,200,000	6,100,000
− Income Tax Liability	844,387	1,088,254
− Mortgage Balance	4,144,940	4,418,287
Net Cash from Sale on Reversion	210,673	593,459

NET PRESENT VALUE OF CASH FLOWS

In table 8.11, the net cash returns on reversion are discounted to obtain their present values, and from the accumulated sum of the present value of the after-tax cash flows (ATCF) and the net cash from sale (NCFS) is subtracted the equity cash outlay to obtain the net present value of the cash flows. Symbolically, the net present value can be expressed in compact notation as follows:

$$\text{net present value} = N_{t=1}\frac{\text{ATCF}}{(1+r)}t + \frac{\text{NCFS}}{(1+r)}N - \frac{\text{equity cash outlay}}{(1+r)^0}, \quad (8.4)$$

which can be expressed in words as

net present value = sum of the discounted value of the yearly after-tax cash flow plus the discounted value of the net cash flow from sale less the equity cash outlay investment,

where r represents the discount rate of return, which the investor requires as the desired return to be earned from the investment. A positive net present value represents the excess discounted cash flow above the cash flow needed to produce the required rate of return. It therefore represents a kind of surplus cash return to the mortgagor.

The net present values are $296,840 for Northridge and $523,310 for Vining. Both properties are profitable and have generated returns substantially above the required rate of return of 9 percent, as reflected in their net present values. The net present value of the Vining property of $523,310 is $226,470 greater than that of $296,840 from the Northridge property. The higher net present value of the Vining property is indicative of its higher rate of profitability.

Table 8.11
Computation of Net Present Value (000's)

	NORTHRIDGE			VINING		
Year	After Tax Cash Flow	Present Value Discount Factor @ 9%	Present Value	After Tax Cash Flow	Present Value Discount Factor @ 9%	Present Value
1987	115.26	0.9174	105.74	141.30	0.9174	129.63
1988	107.67	.8417	90.63	132.70	.8417	111.69
1989	100.25	.7722	77.41	124.25	.7722	95.95
1990	92.98	.7084	65.78	115.92	.7084	82.12
1991	85.83	.6499	55.78	107.68	.6499	69.98
1992	78.79	.5963	46.98	99.50	.5963	59.33
1993	282.48	.5470	154.52	684.84	.5470	374.61
Total P.V. of After Tax Cash Flow			596.84	Total P.V. of After Net Cash Flow		923.31
1986	Cash Outlay (Equity Investment)			Cash Outlay (Equity Investment)		
	-300.00	1.0000	300.00	-400.00	1.0000	-400.00
Net Present Value			296.84	Net Present Value		523.31

THE INTERNAL RATE OF RETURN METHOD

The internal rate of return (IRR) is another indicator of profitability. It is the discount rate that equates the present value of the cash inflows generated by the property to the present value of the equity investment (I) in the property. The cash inflows of the property are the total cash return after reversion (TCR) derived in tables 8.6a and 8.6b. The internal rate of return is defined as follows:

IRR = present value of total cash return − present value of equity investment = 0.

This relationship can be expressed in notational form as

$$\text{IRR} = \frac{\text{TCR}_1}{(1 + R)} + \frac{\text{TCR}_2}{(1 + R)^2} + \frac{\cdots}{111} + \frac{\text{TCR}_N}{(1 + R)^N} - I = 0 = \text{NPV} \qquad (8.5)$$

or

$$\text{IRR} = \sum_{t = 1}^{N} \frac{\text{TCR}_t}{(1 + R)^t} - I = 0 = \text{NPV}.$$

The internal rate of return is obtained when the present value of the cash inflow (total cash return) is equal to the present value of the cash outflow (equity investment). This implies that the net present value is zero at the internal rate of return. The internal rate of return represents one of the cases of the discounted cash flow net present value criterion: NPV = 0 = IRR.

Table 8.12 shows how the internal rate of return is calculated. In equation (8.5), both the total cash returns and the equity investments are known, but the discount rate, R, is unknown. Equation (8.5) can therefore be solved for the one unknown to obtain the value of R that will make the sum of the discounted total cash returns equal to the equity investment, which reduces the equation to zero; this value of R is the internal rate of return.

Using equation (8.5), two approaches can be employed to obtain the internal rate of return: (1) trial and error and (2) direct solution of the equation. The trial and error technique is much simpler and will be presented here. The present value of the total cash returns was derived in table 8.11 using a discount rate of 9 percent, which was the rate of return required by the investor. A positive net present value was obtained for Northridge and Vining when the equity investment was deducted from the sum of the present value of the cash inflows. The positive net present value indicates that a higher discount rate than 9 percent is required to reduce the total cash return to equal the equity investment. In the trial and error process, incremental discount rates are tried until the present value of the total cash return is equal to the equity investment. But this can easily become a tedious process if there are many years involved or if the rate is high.

A discussion of the calculations in table 8.12 illustrates the process of deter-

Table 8.12
Finding the Internal Rate of Return

Year	Net Cash Flow Northridge (000's)	Net Cash Flow Vining (000's)	20 Percent Present Value PVIF	20 Percent Northridge (000's)	20 Percent Vining (000's)	32.5 Percent Present Value PVIF	32.5 Percent Northridge (000's)	32.5 Percent Vining (000's)	33.5 Percent Present Value PVIF	33.5 Percent Northridge (000's)	33.5 Percent Vining (000's)
1	115.26	141.30	0.8065	92.96	113.96	0.7576	87.32	107.05	0.74906	---	105.84
2	107.67	132.70	0.6504	70.03	86.31	0.5739	61.79	76.16	0.56110	---	74.46
3	100.25	124.25	0.5245	52.58	65.18	0.4348	43.57	54.02	0.42030	---	52.22
4	92.98	115.92	0.4230	39.33	49.03	0.3294	30.63	38.18	0.31483	---	36.50
5	85.83	107.68	0.3411	29.28	36.73	0.2495	21.41	26.87	0.23583	---	25.39
6	78.79	99.50	0.2751	21.68	27.37	0.1890	14.89	18.81	0.17666	---	17.58
7	282.48	684.84	0.2218	62.65	151.90	0.1432	40.45	98.07	0.13232	---	90.62
Present Value	865.26	2,127.54		368.51	530.48		300.06	419.16		402.61	402.61
PV/I = A/B	865.26 300	2,127.54 400		368.51 300	530.48 400		300.06 300	419.16 400		402.61	402.61 400
AT IRR: A/B = 1	2.88	5.33		1.228	1.326		1.0	1.048		---	1.007
NPV = PV - I	565.26	1,727.54		68.51	130.48		0.06	19.16		---	0.01
AT IRR: NPV = 0							0.01				0.01

mining the internal rate of return using trial and error. From equation (8.5), the following statements can be made:

At the internal rate of return, R

1. The net present value equals zero. Then:

(a) If NPV > 0, the discount rate (r) is below the IRR: $r < R$.
(b) If NPV < 0, the discount rate (r) is higher than the IRR: $r > R$.

2. The present value of the cash inflows (A) is equal to the present value of the cash outflows (B), which means $A = B$; and this implies that $A/B = 1$. Then:

(a) If $A/B > 1$, the discount rate (r) is lower than the IRR: $r < R$.
(b) If $A/B < 1$, the discount rate (r) is higher than the IRR: $r > R$.

The two indicators above give the direction in which to proceed in finding the IRR. As would be observed, these indicators give the same direction and should be used as alternatives. In table 8.12, both are presented to demonstrate how to use them. From table 8.11, the net present values using a 9 percent discount rate are $296,840 for Northridge and $523,310 for Vining.

Since the Northridge NPV is $296,840 and the cash outflow (equity investment) is $300,000, this indicates the IRR is significantly different from the discount rate of 9 percent. Similarly, the Vining NPV of $523,310 is greater than the cash outflow of $400,000, and the IRR for Vining will be even greater.

Using the second indicator,

$$\text{Northridge:} \quad A/B = \frac{596.84}{300.00} = 1.99 \text{ times.}$$

$$\text{Vining:} \quad A/B = \frac{923.31}{400.00} = 2.31 \text{ -times.}$$

The indicators for both properties show that the IRR is much larger than 9 percent. The magnitude of the difference indicates a significantly higher IRR for either project.

In the first iteration, 20 percent is used, which is more than two times as large as 9 percent, and the indicators show that the difference between the NPV(A) and the equity investment (B) has narrowed but is still substantially different. In the second iteration, 32.5 percent is used; A/B for Northridge is approximately 1.000, which is the IRR for Northridge; but Vining still has some small difference, since A/B is greater than one. In the third iteration, 33.5 percent is the approximate IRR for Vining. Although the indicators are not at the exact point, the difference is minute.

The internal rate of return obtained for each project is 32.5 percent for Northridge and 33.5 percent for Vining.

From a comparison of the net present values of the two properties (Northridge: $296,840; Vining: $523,310), it would appear that the Vining property is substantially more profitable than the Northridge property. The cash throw-off of Vining is significantly greater than that of Northridge, and is much more profitable. But a substantial part of the cash from the Vining property came from reversion at the end of the seven-year holding period and is not worth as much as when measured at the outset of the investment. In other words, the timing of the cash flows is very important in discounting. The big terminal cash inflow from Vining is not available for reinvestment during the life of the project, and its impact on the IRR is minimal. Hence, the internal rate of return of Vining is only one percentage point higher than that of Northridge.

It should be pointed out that the IRR assumes that the cash throw-off in each period is reinvested at the internal rate of return. If this assumption is violated, the property will not yield the internal rate of return over the holding period.

RANKING: NET PRESENT VALUE VERSUS INTERNAL RATE OF RETURN CRITERIA

In the above analysis, both the net present value and the internal rate of return gave the same ranking, showing Vining a more profitable and attractive investment than Northridge. The net present value and the internal rate of return give the same accept/reject decisions for projects in general. Some instances when the two methods rank projects differently are (1) when the cost of one project is significantly larger than the cost of the other and (2) when the timing of the projects cash flows differs, for example, when the cash flows of one project increase over time while those of the other project decrease or when the projects have different lives.

What would be the tax implication if a foreclosure should occur during the expected holding period before reversion? The analysis presented in table 8.13 shows what this would be. When the lender forecloses on a property, legal action is taken to assume control over the property, and the lender proceeds to dispose of it to recover the mortgage balance. The tax authorities use the mortgage balance as the sale price for the property at the time of foreclosure. A tax liability results if the mortgage balance exceeds the net book value. The difference between the unpaid mortgage balance, which becomes the sale price for tax purposes, and the net book value is the taxable gain at foreclosure computed for each of the years of the holding period. In the year of purchase, there is no taxable gain on foreclosure, since the net book value is the purchase price that exceeds the unpaid mortgage balance by the amount of the equity invested in the property. There is also no taxable gain on foreclosure in the first year because the net book value is still higher than the unpaid mortgage. From the second year onward, the higher accelerated depreciation rate causes the net book value to fall faster than the unpaid mortgage balance, resulting in taxable gain on foreclosure.

This tax effect is important to the lender since the tax due will be paid from the foreclosure sale proceeds before the unpaid mortgage balance is paid off. This means that in the event of foreclosure, the lender should try to get a price high

Table 8.13
Tax Effects if Foreclosure Occurs ($000's)

	NORTHRIDGE			VINING		
	Unpaid Mortgage Balance	Net Book Value	Taxable Gain on Foreclosure	Unpaid Mortgage Balance	Net Book Value	Taxable Gain on Foreclosure
1986	4,500.00	4,800.00	—	4,900.00	5,150.00	—
1987	4,460.00	4,560.00	—	4,846.00	4,892.50	—
1988	4,417.32	4,332.00	85.32	4,787.68	4,647.88	139.80
1989	4,370.56	4,115.40	255.16	4,724.79	4,415.49	309.30
1990	4,320.49	3,909.63	410.86	4,656.79	4,194.72	462.05
1991	4,266.41	3,714.15	552.26	4,583.30	3,984.97	598.33
1992	4,208.01	3,528.44	679.57	4,503.96	3,785.72	719.24
1993	4,144.94	3,352.02	792.92	4,418.27	3,596.43	821.84

Table 8.14
Decomposition of Cash Flow Benefits and Tax Liability on Reversion (000's)

		Northridge		Vining	
		$ Amount	%	$ Amount	%
1.	Recapture of Mortgage Amortization	355.06	16.83	481.73	14.32
2.	Increase in Sales Price	400.00	18.96	800.00	23.79
3.	Past Depreciation Tax Recapture	(303.99)	14.41	(326.16)	9.70
4.	Return of Initial Cash	300.00	14.22	400.00	11.89
5.	Tax on Capital Gains	(540.40)	25.61	(762.09)	22.66
6.	Net Cash from Sale at Reversion	210.67	9.98	593.48	17.64

enough to cover both the final tax liability on the taxable gain and the unpaid balance. When the real estate market is depressed, the lender may, when possible, try to avoid or delay foreclosure, if the sale price might not be sufficient to meet the final obligations.

Table 8.14 shows the decomposition of the cash flow benefits that will accrue to the investor, the income tax liability due, and their proportional relationship to the aggregate cash flow on reversion of the property at the end of the holding period. The net cash from sale on reversion obtained here is the residual cash flow due to the investor when the property is sold, and it reconciles with the data in table 8.10. This net cash is received at closing and is in addition to the after-tax cash flows of each of the seven years before reversion.

The items in table 8.14 are obtained from a variety of sources. The recapture of mortgage amortization represents the sum of the yearly amortization shown in line 5 of tables 8.6a and 8.6b. The appreciation in the property value from the date of purchase to the date of sale is shown as the increase in sales price, representing the difference between the sale price and the purchase price shown in lines 14 and 2, respectively, of table 8.2. The tax recapture of the excess accelerated depreciation taken, above the equivalent straight line depreciation amounts at reversion shown in line 3, is obtained from table 8.8. The investor's equity, line 3 of table 8.2, is returned on reversion as shown in line 4. The tax on any capital gain from the sale of the property must be accounted for as a cash outflow, before the net cash flow due the investor is derived.

The sum of the two tax items in table 8.14, past depreciation tax recapture and tax on capital gains, equals the amount of income tax liability in table 8.10. Note that the income tax liability is deducted from the sale proceeds before the mortgage balance is paid. It is therefore of importance to the lender to examine the elements that make up the cash flows on reversion, to assess potential risk exposure.

An examination of table 8.14 shows that recapture of mortgage amortization made up a higher proportion of the cash flows of Northridge than Vining. The price appreciation factor for Vining was twice that of Northridge. The tax liability for depreciation recapture and capital gains made up a higher proportion of the cash flows of Northridge than Vining, which is reflected in the higher net cash flow of Vining relative to Northridge.

NOTE

1. The new tax code was still going through Congress at the time these computations were done. Since it was not definite what the new lower tax rates would actually be prior to completion of the tax bill, the current rate of 50 percent is used.

Index